STUDIES IN AFRICAN MUSIC

VOLUME II

Studies in African Music, Volume II, contains the music dealt
with in the text of Volume I

A. M. JONES

STUDIES IN

AFRICAN MUSIC

VOLUME II

LONDON

OXFORD UNIVERSITY PRESS

NEW YORK   TORONTO   CAPE TOWN

Oxford University Press, Ely House, London W. 1

GLASGOW NEW YORK TORONTO MELBOURNE WELLINGTON
CAPE TOWN IBADAN NAIROBI DAR ES SALAAM LUSAKA ADDIS ABABA
DELHI BOMBAY CALCUTTA MADRAS KARACHI LAHORE DACCA
KUALA LUMPUR SINGAPORE HONG KONG TOKYO

ISBN 0 19 713512 9

First Edition 1959
Reprinted 1962, 1969 *and* 1971

PRINTED IN GREAT BRITAIN

CONTENTS

INTRODUCTION   *Page* vii

NOTE   ,, viii

1. PLAY-SONGS AND FISHING SONGS   Eve Tribe   ,,   1

2. THE NYAYITO DANCE   ,,   ,, 11

3. YEVE CULT MUSIC:

   a. THE HUSAGO DANCE   ,,   ,, 41

   b. THE SOVU DANCE   ,,   ,, 77

   c. THE SOGBA DANCE   ,,   ,, 93

4. THE ADZIDA DANCE   ,,   ,, 112

5. THE AGBADZA DANCE   ,,   ,, 166

6. THE ICILA DANCE   Lala Tribe   ,, 218

APPENDIX: Two Independent Corroborators   ,, 237

INTRODUCTION

THE main purpose of this book is to provide musicians with some examples of African dance music printed in Full Score and *in extenso*. As far as we know, it is the first book of its kind.

It forms the second volume of a single work and will not be intelligible to Western musicians without the detailed discussions and commentaries which will be found in Volume I.

In reading the more intricate passages of the score it will probably be found helpful to have at hand a transparent ruler, or better still a transparent set-square, one edge of which may be placed vertically down the music. By sliding this across the page, the student will be able to see with exactitude how the various rhythms fall with respect to each other.

Anyone ought, with sufficient practice, to be able to perform the Play-Songs and Fishing Songs. But the drumming is a different matter: while a good Ewe musician, once he has heard the Nonsense Syllables, would be able to reproduce the drum patterns, we Western people would need a tablature indicating the hands used for each beat, together with the type of beat to be made. It is impossible to include all this on a readable Full Score. Yet the amateur enthusiast has not been left entirely unsatisfied. At the back of Volume I he will find performance scores of some of the music in the present book. With the information there provided, and with the help of the Full Scores, he has the requisite technical instructions to be able to attempt the thrilling exercise of playing African cross-rhythms, in which we wish him all success.

For far too long African dance music—and that means the flower of the African musical tradition—has lain under the hazy mists of qualitative description. In this volume we have attempted to let it emerge into the clear light, so that it can be seen for what it is and thus make its bow to the musical world.

We acknowledge with gratitude the generous grant made by the School of Oriental and African Studies to meet the cost of the publication of this book.

A. M. JONES

School of Oriental and African Studies,
University of London
May 1956

NOTE

WHEN the drums are playing together, the sound does not strike the ear as a series of chords: their notes are not sufficiently precise to produce this effect: the rise and fall of the several drum-tunes remain unblended in the mind. So in reading these scores it must be remembered that:

1. Read vertically they show, not a series of chords, but a series of rhythmic relationships.

2. Read horizontally, however, each stave shows the rise and fall of the tune in the normal way.

Key Signatures

1. The Bell staves show the actual pitches played.

2. The Rattle makes two sharp high sounds of indeterminate pitch, at least a fifth apart. The pitch of the notes given on the stave is arbitrary and chosen for convenience.

3. Songs.

Though normal Key Signatures are used to facilitate reading the score, they must not be taken to mean that the African has the same feeling for 'Key' as Western music has.

4. The Drums.

The bracketed sharps and flats placed where Western music puts a Key Signature are not Key Signatures in the Western sense. While they indicate that the notes affected are sharpened or flattened right through the piece unless accidentals occur, they do not indicate any tonality. Further, they indicate the special tuning of the drum for the particular dance.

For details see Vol. I, Chapter III

PLAY SONGS FOR CHILDREN and FISHING SONGS

Eʋe Tribe — Ghana

PLAY SONGS

Song 1

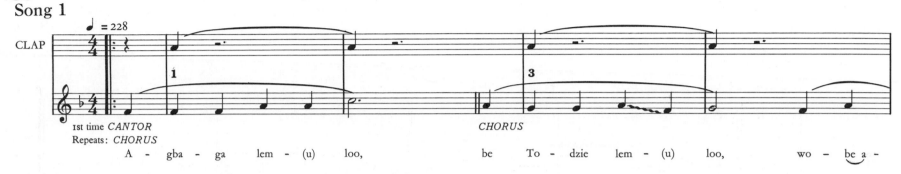

1st time CANTOR
Repeats: CHORUS

A - gba - ga lem - (u) loo, be To - dzie lem - (u) loo, wo - be a -

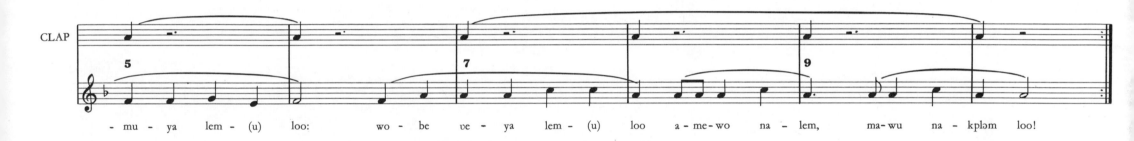

- mu - ya lem - (u) loo: wo - be ʋe - ya lem - (u) loo a - me - wo na - lem, ma - wu na - kplɔm loo!

Song 2

[Clap NOT used in practice]

etc. CANTOR CHORUS CANTOR CHOR. CANTOR CHORUS
Tɔ - me - lo le, Ee, Go - ta - lo le, Ee, Sukuviwo - mi - fu du, gba - sa - srã, gba - sa - srã!

I

PLAY SONGS

Song 3

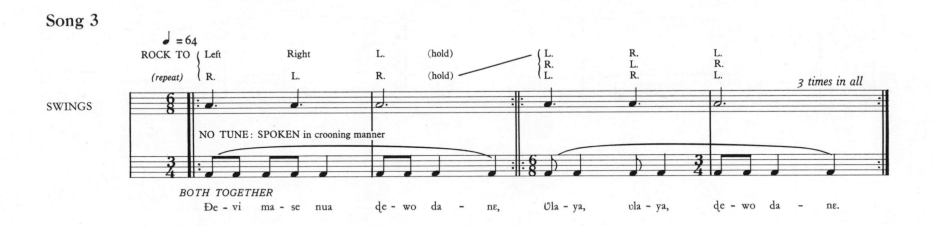

ROCK TO { Left   Right   L.   (hold)   { L.   R.   L.
(repeat) { R.   L.   R.   (hold)   { R.   L.   R.
                                                 { L.   R.   L.

SWINGS

3 times in all

NO TUNE: SPOKEN in crooning manner

BOTH TOGETHER
Đe - vi   ma - se   nua   đe - wo   da —   nɛ,   ʊla - ya,   ʊla - ya,   đe - wo   da —   nɛ.

Song 4

CLAP 1

CLAP 2

1

3

5

CANTOR
A - hiã - via   ye - ye,   Tsoe   da   đe   a - ba - tia   dzi   nam-(u)   loo,

CHORUS
A - hiã - via   gbɔ - gbɔ,   tsoe   da   đe   a - ba - tia   dzi   nam-(u)   loo.

2

PLAY SONGS

Song 5

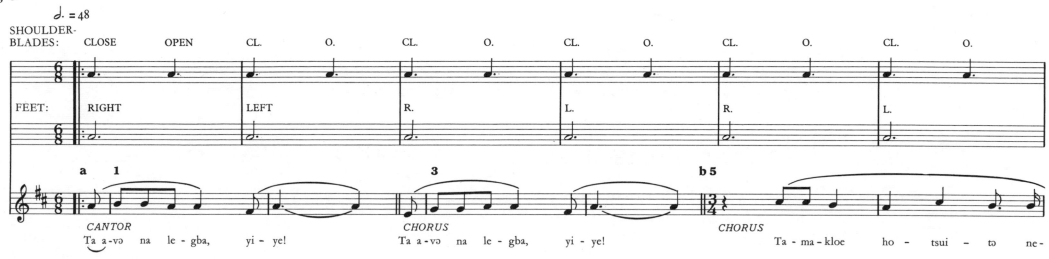

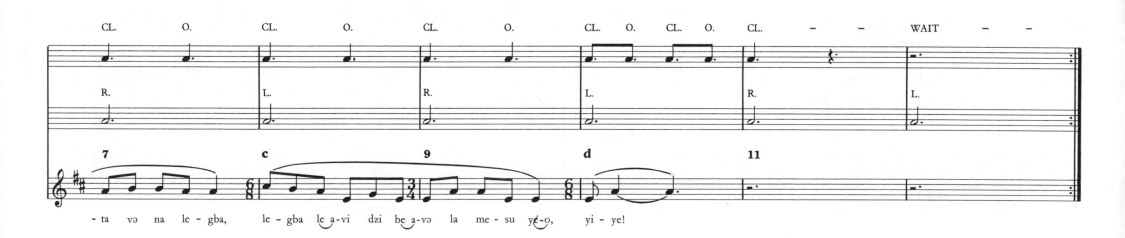

PLAY SONGS

SONG 6

♩ = 120

CLAP 2 is not used in performance (see text)

A – ba – ye loo, A – ba – ye, Ku – nu ba – yee, A – ya ḍu gbe,

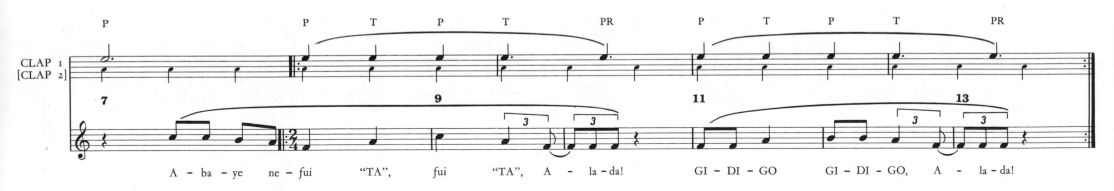

A – ba – ye ne – fui "TA", fui "TA", A – la – da! GI – DI – GO GI – DI – GO, A – la – da!

P = Left palm upwards and right palm downwards on partner's hands.
T = Clap your *own* hands together.
PR = Left palm downwards and right palm upwards on partner's hands.
E = Right elbow on left palm of partner.

PLAY SONGS

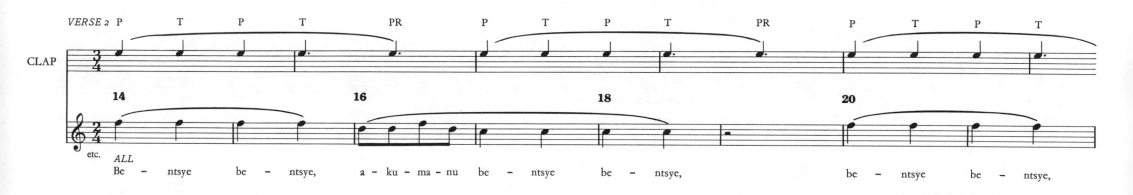

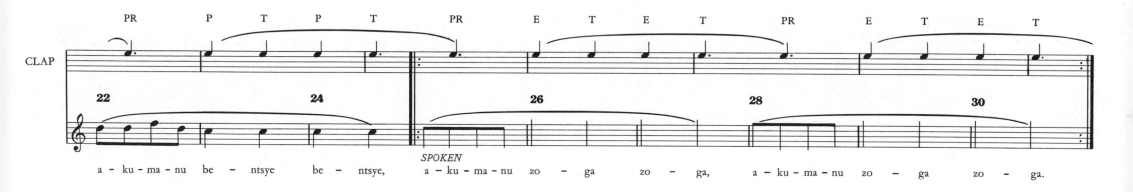

PLAY SONGS

SONG 7

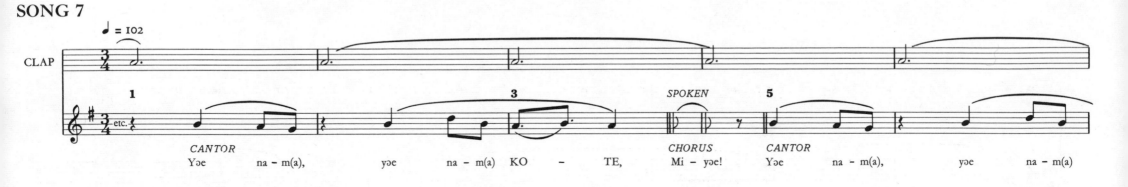

CANTOR Yɔe na – m(a), yɔe na – m(a) KO – TE, Mi – yɔe! Yɔe na – m(a), yɔe na – m(a)

CHORUS CANTOR

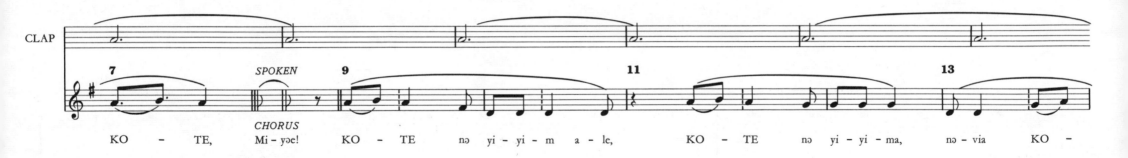

KO – TE, Mi – yɔe! KO – TE nɔ yi – yi – m a – le, KO – TE nɔ yi – yi – ma, nɔ – via KO –

CHORUS

– LE he – kploe ɖo, wo – be nu – wɔ – nue le ye wɔm, Mi – yɔe!

6

PLAY SONGS

SONG 8

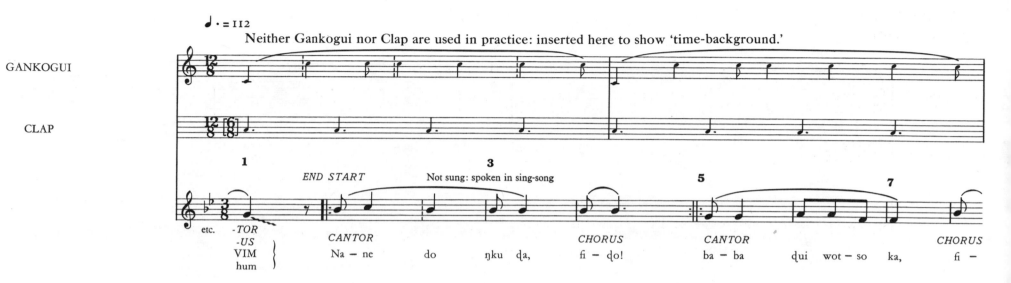

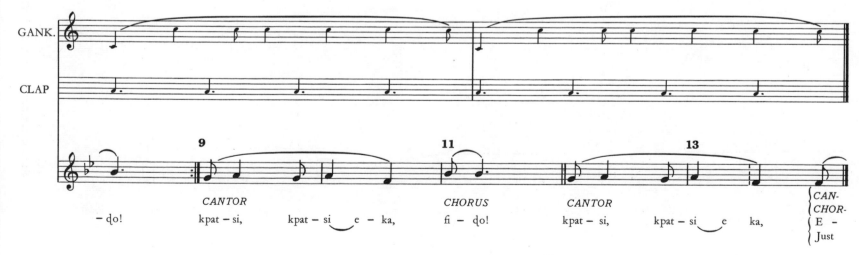

PLAY SONGS FOR CHILDREN and FISHING SONGS

FISHING SONGS
1. Sprat-catching

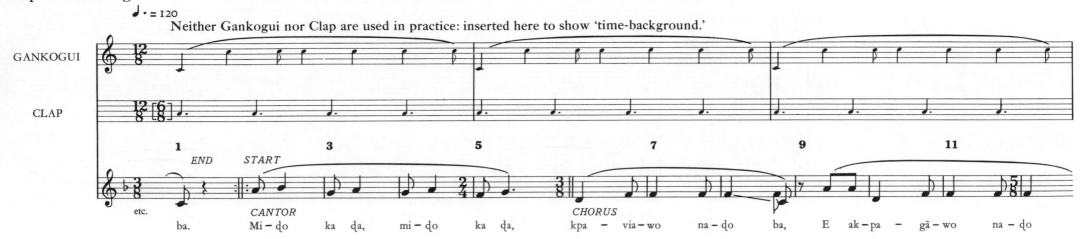

Neither Gankogui nor Clap are used in practice: inserted here to show 'time-background.'

ba. Mi – do ka da, mi – do ka da, kpa – via – wo na – do ba, E ak – pa – gã – wo na – do

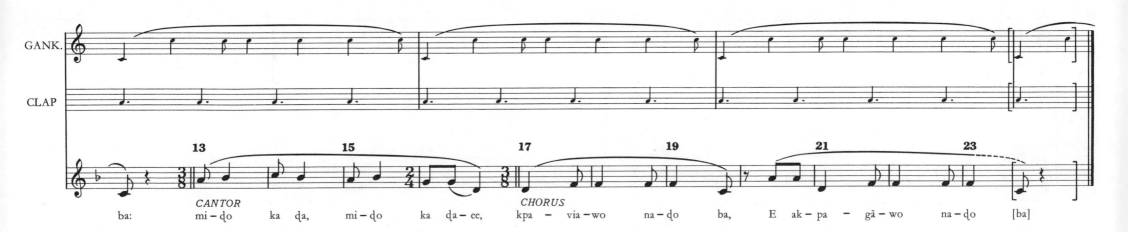

ba: mi – do ka da, mi – do ka da – ee, kpa – via – wo na – do ba, E ak – pa – gã – wo na – do [ba]

FISHING SONGS

2. Paddle Song

♩ = 120

Gankogui is not used in practice

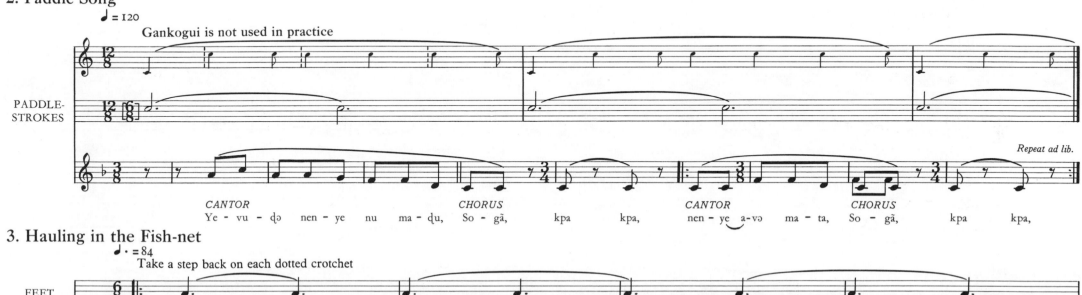

PADDLE-STROKES

Repeat ad lib.

CANTOR
Ye - vu - ɖɔ nen - ye nu ma - ɖu, So - gã, kpa kpa, nen - ye a-vɔ ma - ta, So - gã, kpa kpa,

3. Hauling in the Fish-net

♩· = 84

Take a step back on each dotted crotchet

FEET

CANTOR
A - lã - ga - wo gbɔ - na, so - lã - ga - wo gbɔ - na ɖa, kli - ya kli - ya a - lã - ga - wo gbɔ - na: a -

FEET

CHORUS
- lã - ga - wo gbɔ - na, so - lã - ga - wo gbɔ - na ɖa, kli - ya kli ya so - lã - ga - wo gbɔ - na.

B

FISHING SONGS

4. Fish-collecting Song

NYAYITO DANCE

Mourning

Ewe tribe — Ghana

GANKOGUI

AXATSE

CLAPS

SONG

MASTER DRUM
ATSIMEVU

SOGO

KIDI

KAGAD

CANTOR   *CHORUS*

Vuaviawo,   Beb - le   tsi - tsi - e   me - nye,   nye la   ge - dea - wo   do - mee   ma -

II

NYAYITO DANCE

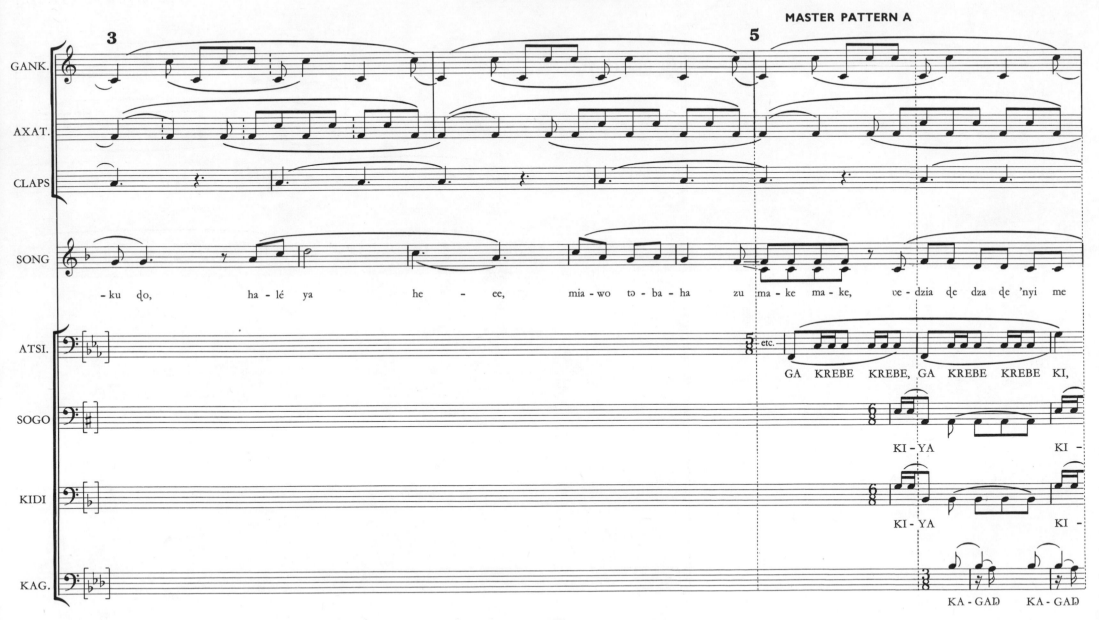

12

NYAYITO DANCE

NYAYITO DANCE

NYAYITO DANCE

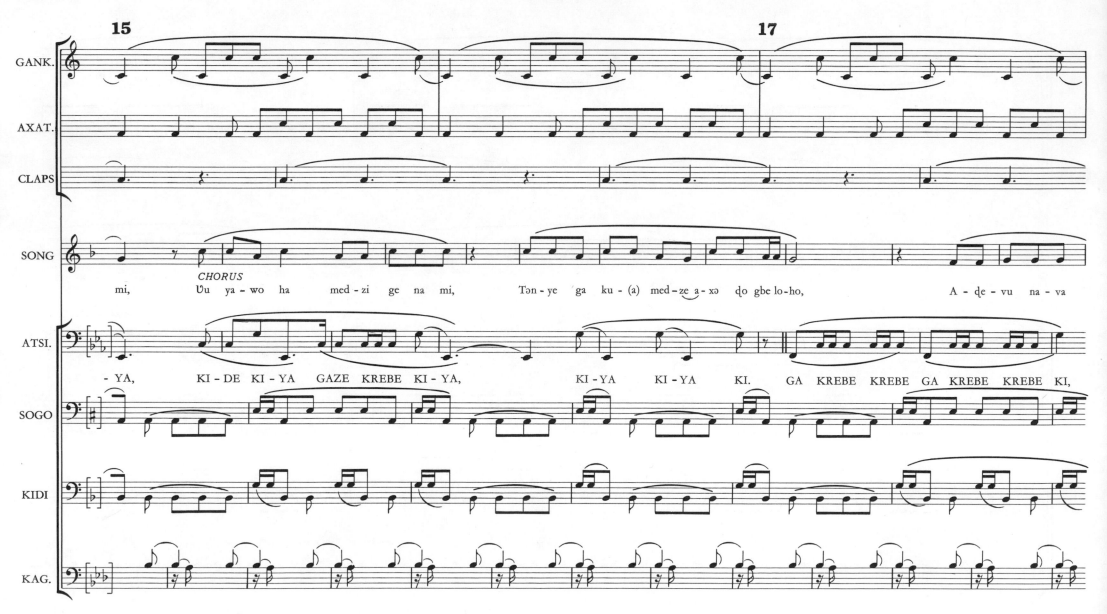

NYAYITO DANCE

CHANGING SIGNAL I

NYAYITO DANCE

NYAYITO DANCE

NYAYITO DANCE

NYAYITO DANCE

NYAYITO DANCE

NYAYITO DANCE

23

NYAYITO DANCE

NYAYITO DANCE

NYAYITO DANCE

NYAYITO DANCE

27

NYAYITO DANCE

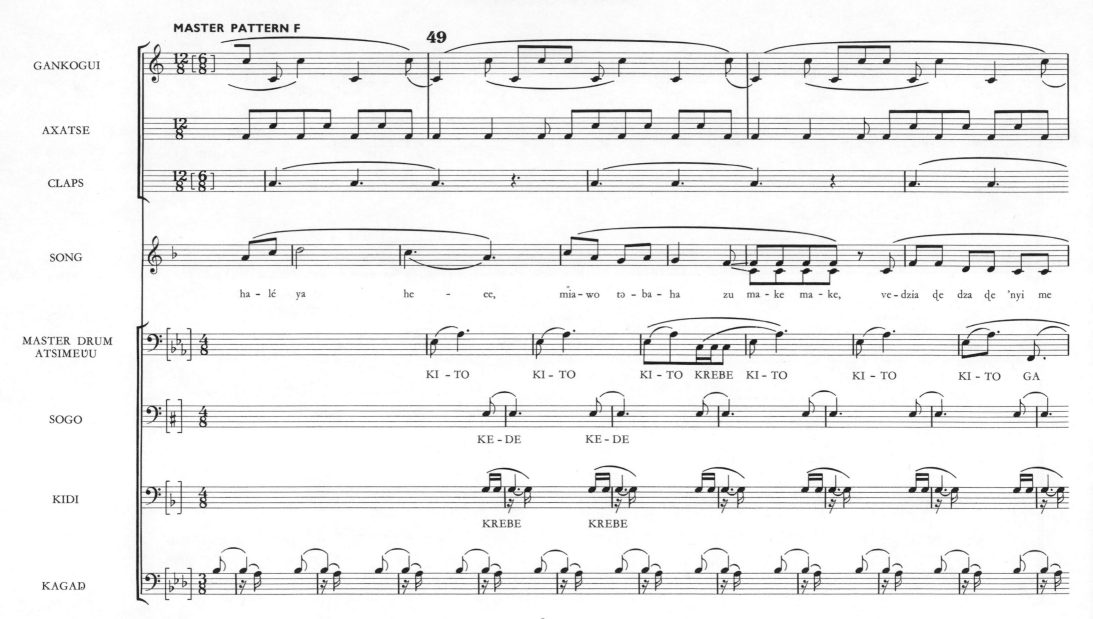

28

NYAYITO DANCE

NYAYITO DANCE

ALTERNATIVE FORMS OF MASTER PATTERN F

GANKOGUI

3 BEATS IN EACH
GANKOGUI PHRASE

MASTER DRUM ATSIMEƲU
STANDARD FORM
OF PATTERN F

KI - TO   KI - TO   KI - TO KREBE KI - TO,   KI - TO   KI - TO   GA

ALTERNATIVE 1.

KI - TO KREBE, KI - TO KREBE, KI - TO KREBE, KI - TOKI - TOKI KI - TOKI - TOKI KI - TOKI - TOKI,

ALTERNATIVE 2.

KI - TO   KI - TO   KI - TO - GAA - GA KI - TO,   KI - TO   KI - TO - GAA - GA
REPEAT

ALTERNATIVE 3.

GA - GA KI - TO, GA - GA KI - TO, GA - GA   KITO, GA - GA KI - TO GA - GA KI - TO, GA - GA   KITO.

ALTERNATIVE 4.

TƆ - TE TEGA - GA, TƆ - TE TEGA - GA, TƆ - TE TEGA - GA KI - TO,   GA - GA,   KI - TO - TO

30

NYAYITO DANCE

NYAYITO DANCE

NYAYITO DANCE

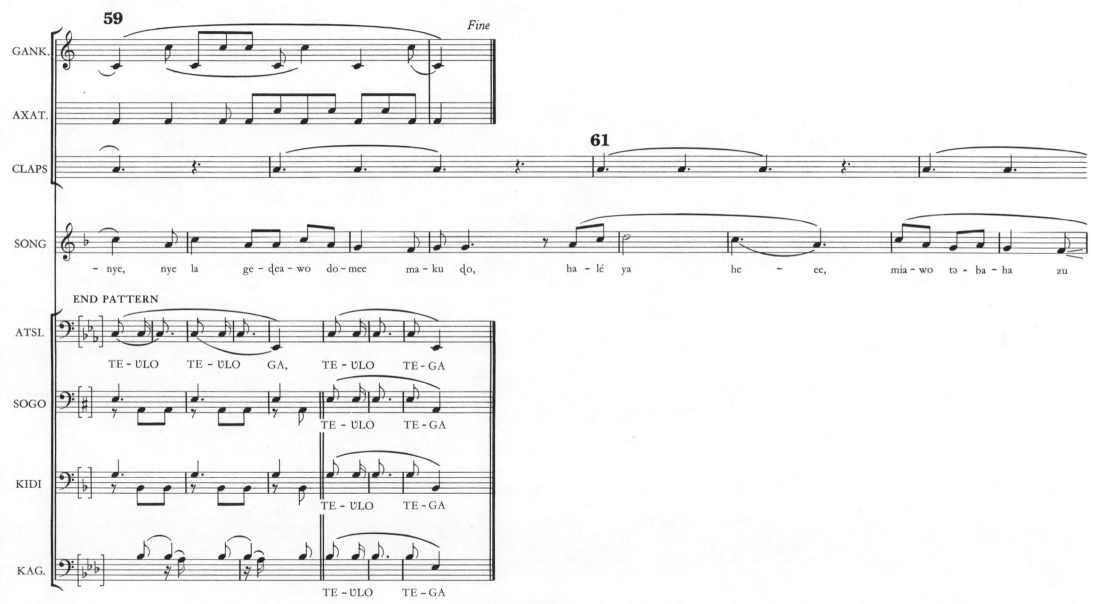

NYAYITO DANCE

NYAYITO DANCE

NYAYITO DANCE

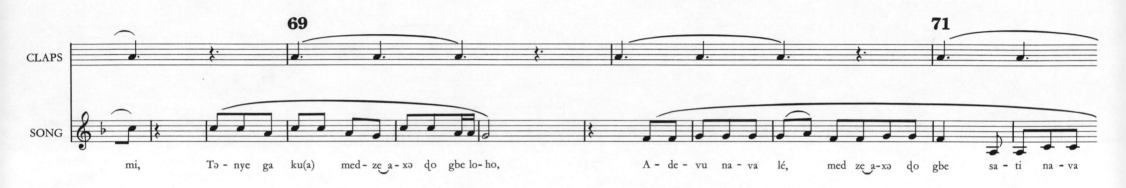

NYAYITO DANCE

CLAPS

73

SONG

CANTOR

tsɔ. Megbloe na mi be med - zi ge na mi,

CHORUS

Ʋu ya - wo ha med - zi ge na mi, Tɔ - nye ga ku (a) me - dze a - xɔ ɖo

NYAYITO DANCE

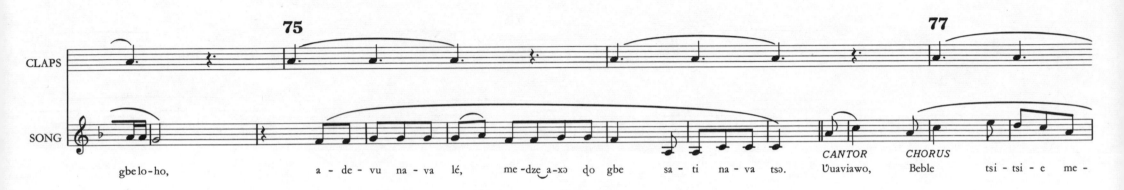

NYAYITO DANCE

CLAPS

SONG

- nye,   nye la   ge - ɖea - wo do - meé   ma - ku ɖo,   ha - lé ya   he — ee,   mia - wo tɔ - ba - ha   zu

NYAYITO DANCE

ma – ke   ma – ke,   ve – dzia ɖe dza ɖe 'nyi me ʋe – nu,   Anyakoawo   yi a – dza wu ge na a – kpa – lu – ee,   ma – do a – lɔewɔ   gbe na mi dzro.

HUSAGO DANCE

Eʋe tribe – Ghana

YEƲE CULT SIGNAL

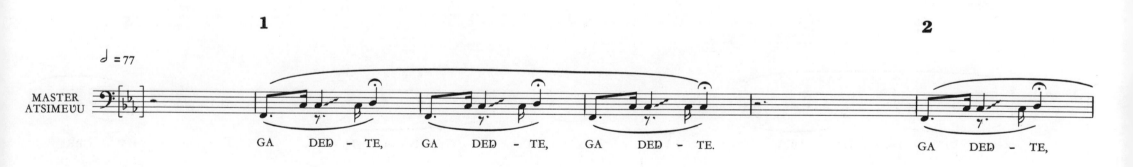

HUSAGO DANCE

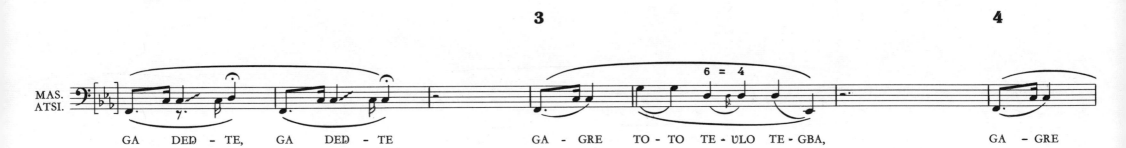

HUSAGO DANCE

HUSAGO DANCE

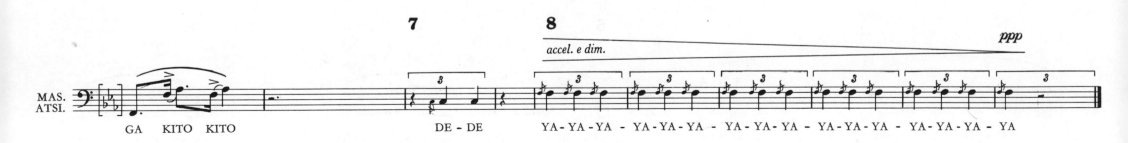

HUSAGO DANCE

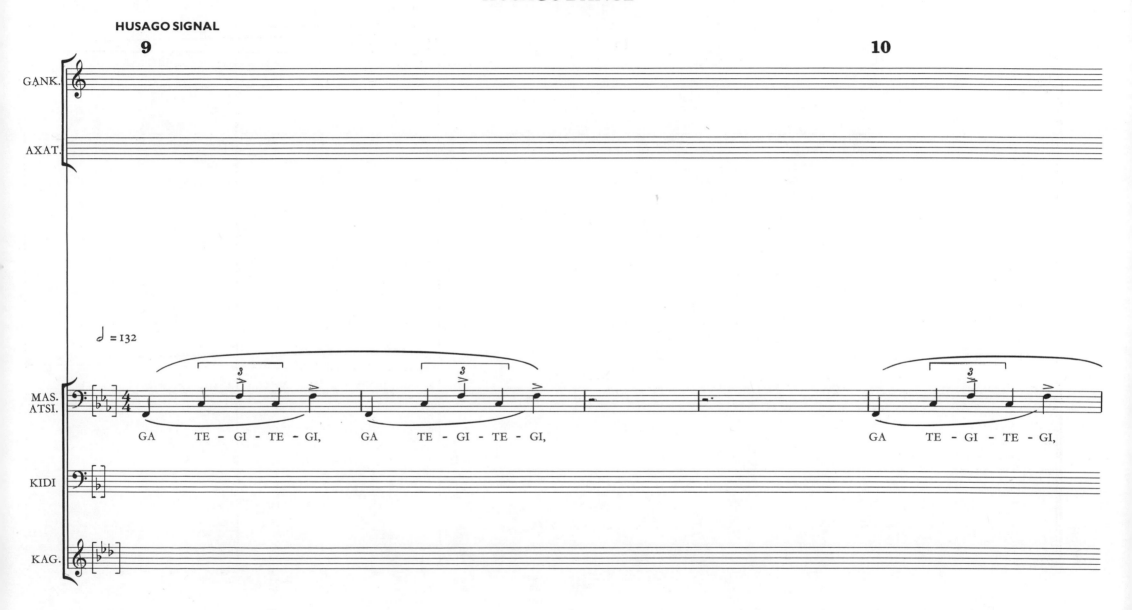

HUSAGO DANCE

HUSAGO DANCE

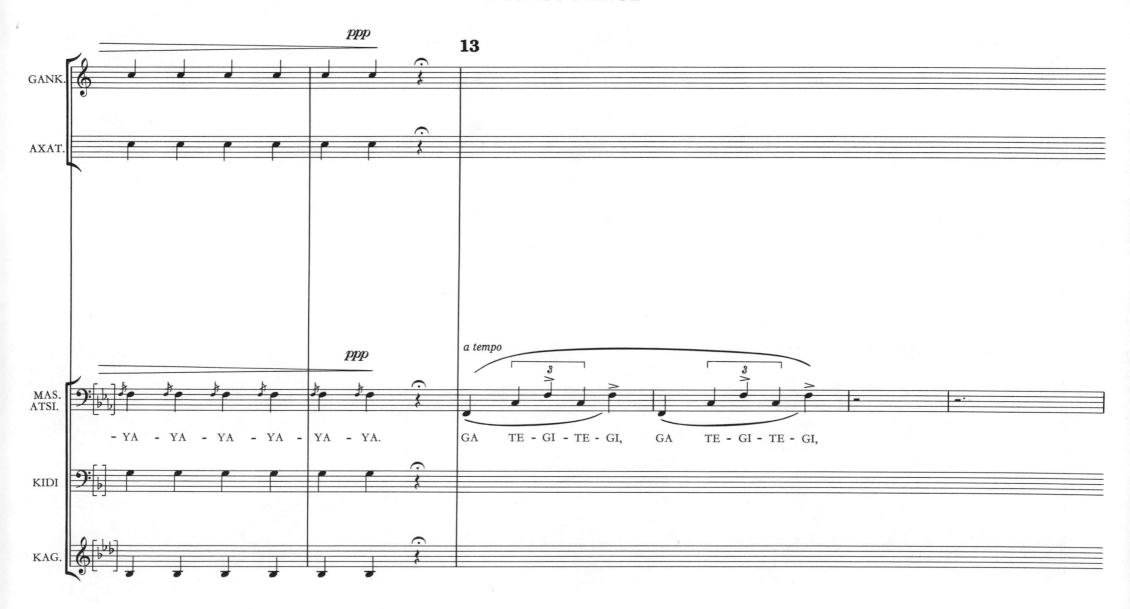

HUSAGO DANCE

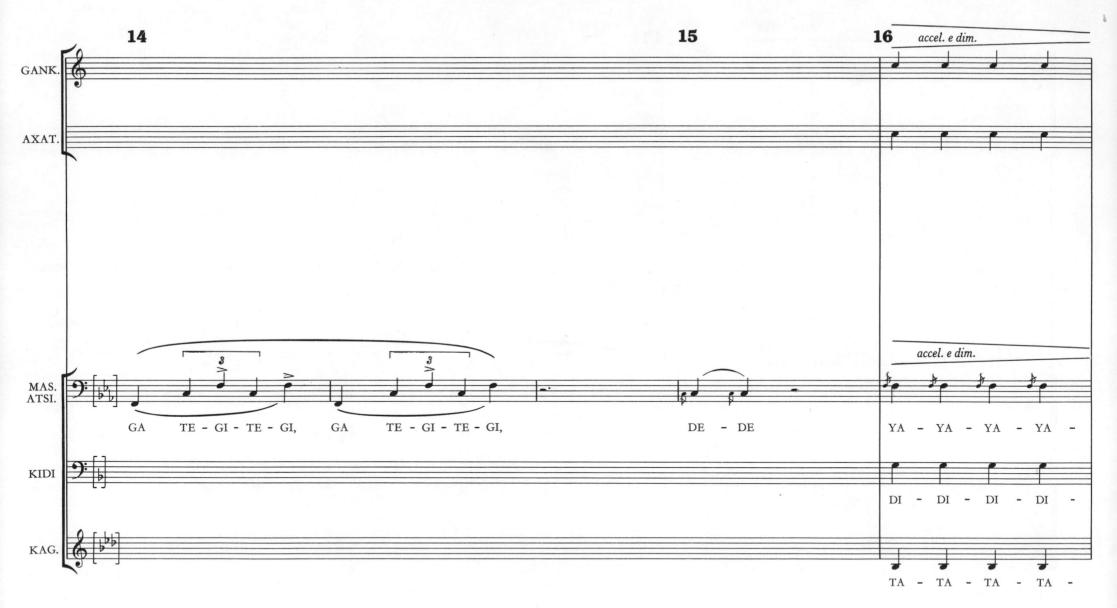

HUSAGO DANCE

HUSAGO DANCE

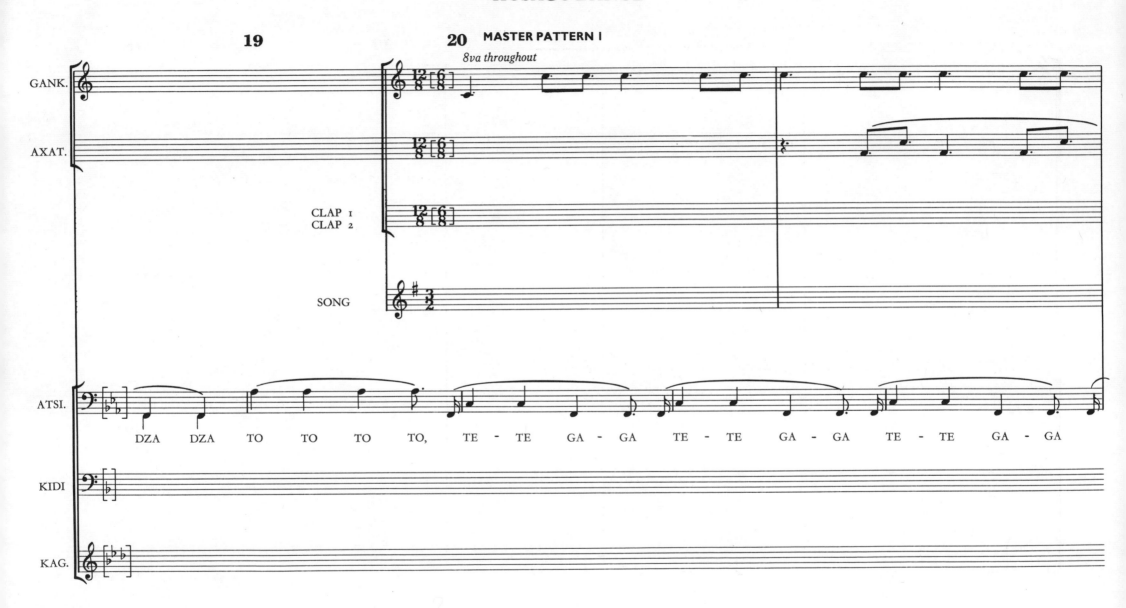

HUSAGO DANCE

HUSAGO DANCE

26

CANTOR
Gbe - dzia do loo - ee, gbe - dzia

HUSAGO DANCE

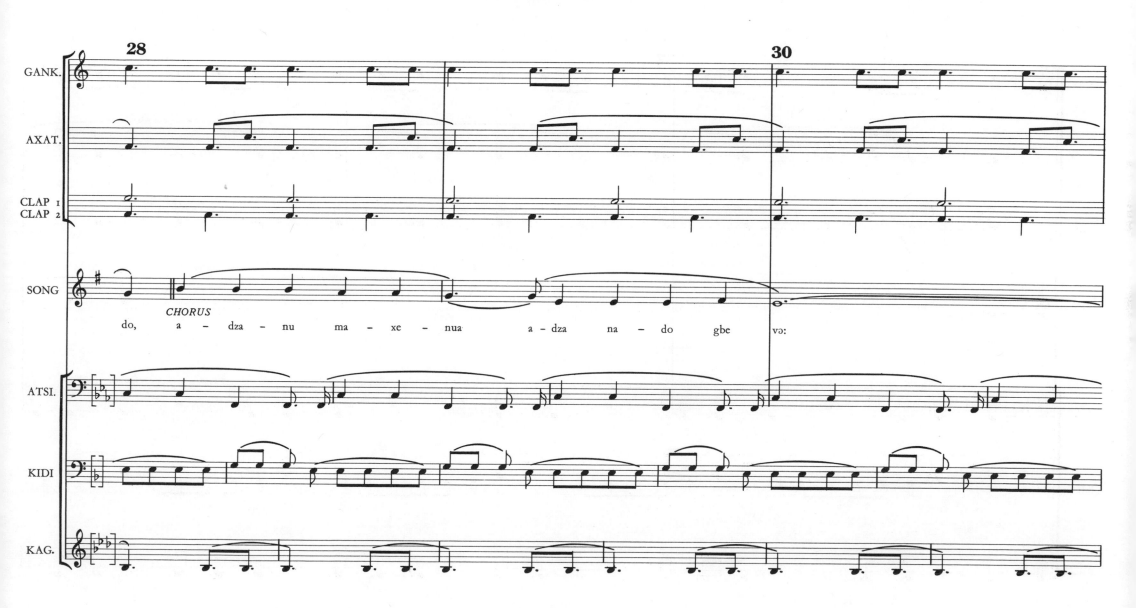

do, a — dza — nu ma — xe — nua a — dza na — do gbe vɔ:

HUSAGO DANCE

HUSAGO DANCE

HUSAGO DANCE

HUSAGO DANCE

vɔ,   "Ka   xo - xowo   nu   wo - gbea   ka   ye - yea - wo   ɖo,"   dza - dza

E

HUSAGO DANCE

HUSAGO DANCE

HUSAGO DANCE

HUSAGO DANCE

HUSAGO DANCE

HUSAGO DANCE

HUSAGO DANCE

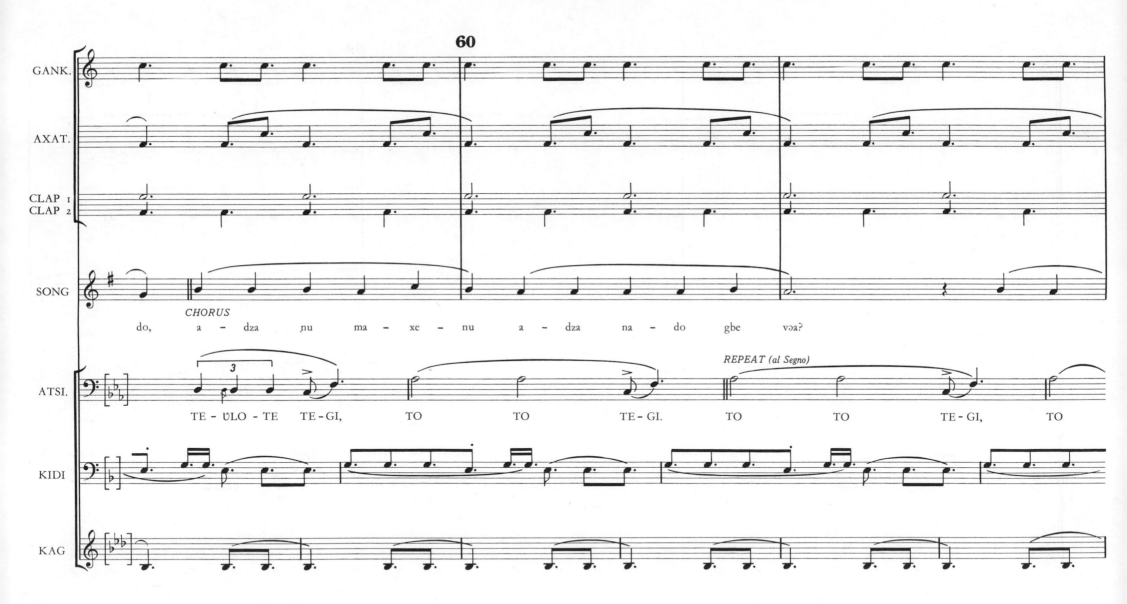

HUSAGO DANCE

HUSAGO DANCE

HUSAGO DANCE

HUSAGO DANCE

HUSAGO DANCE

HUSAGO DANCE

HUSAGO DANCE

HUSAGO DANCE

HUSAGO DANCE

F

HUSAGO DANCE

HUSAGO DANCE

HUSAGO DANCE

*Go on till the
end of
the
verse*

76

SOVU DANCE

Yeve Cult

Eve Tribe—Ghana

SOVU DANCE

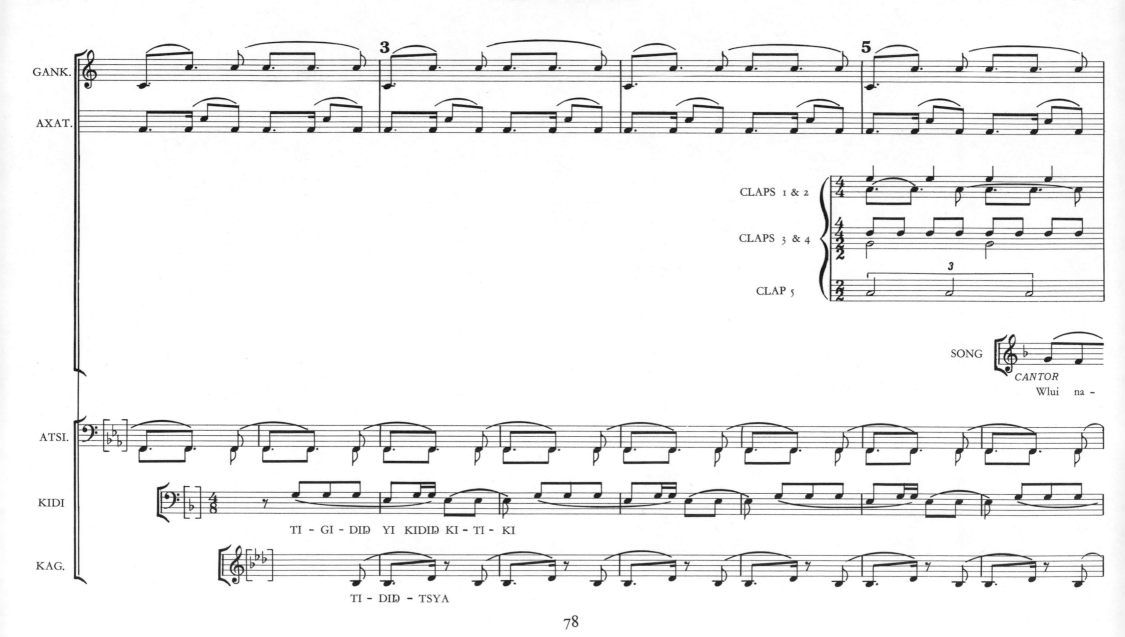

SOVU DANCE

SOVU DANCE

SOVU DANCE

SOVU DANCE

SOVU DANCE

83

SOVU DANCE

84

SOVU DANCE

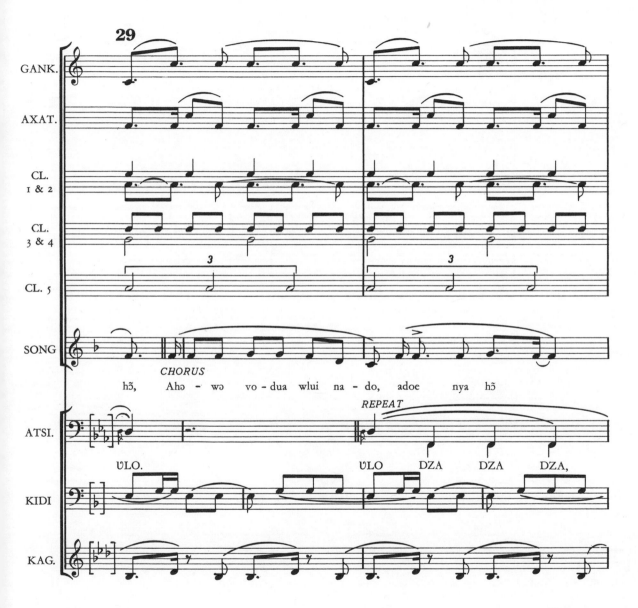

SOVU DANCE

SOVU DANCE

SOVU DANCE

SOVU DANCE

SOVU DANCE

SOVU DANCE

SOVU DANCE

SOGBA or SOGO DANCE

Yeve Cult

SOGBA [or SOGO] SIGNAL

SOGBA or SOGO DANCE

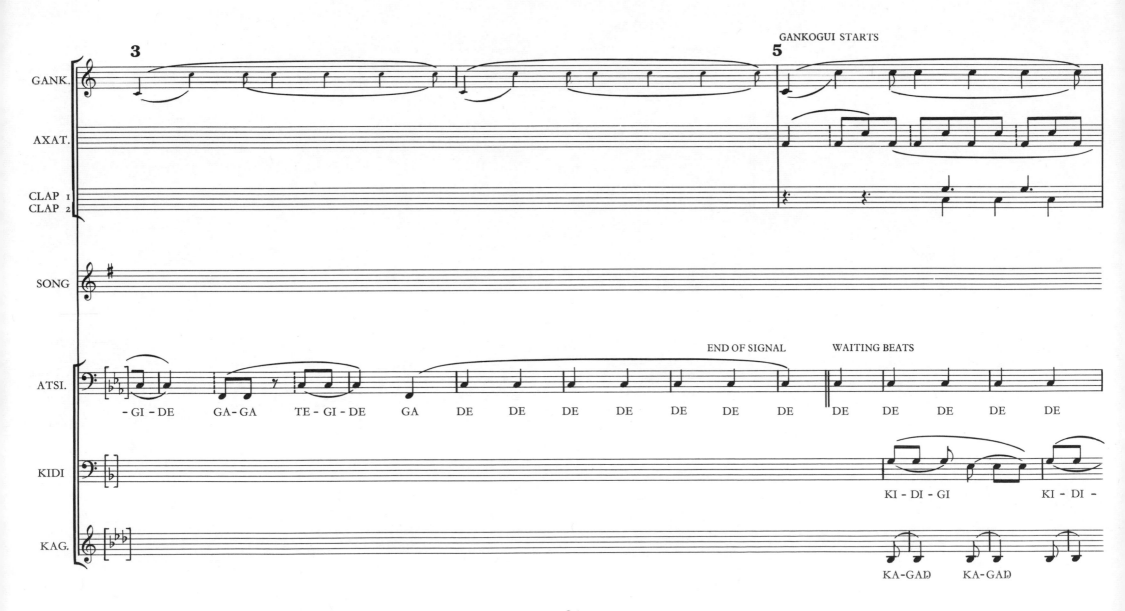

SOGBA or SOGO DANCE

95

SOGBA or SOGO DANCE

SOGBA or SOGO DANCE

SOGBA or SOGO DANCE

SOGBA or SOGO DANCE

99

SOGBA or SOGO DANCE

PATTERN B
21

SOGBA or SOGO DANCE

SOGBA or SOGO DANCE

SOGBA or SOGO DANCE

SOGBA or SOGO DANCE

SOGBA or SOGO DANCE

SOGBA or SOGO DANCE

SOGBA or SOGO DANCE

SOGBA or SOGO DANCE

43

SOGBA or SOGO DANCE

SOGBA or SOGO DANCE

ENDING PATTERN

49

GANKOGUI

AXATSE

CLAP 1
CLAP 2

SONG

nya - nya - te, *CHORUS* Ma - wɔ dza, ma - ku dza, *CANTOR* So - vi A - gba - de - a du

MASTER DRUM
ATSIMEVU

-DZA TO TO - TO. DE-DE-GI DE-DE-GI DE-DE-GI, A -

KIDI

KID KID KID

KAGAÐ

KA - GAÐ KA - GAÐ - - -

110

SOGBA or SOGO DANCE

III

ADZIDA DANCE

Eʋe Tribe — Ghana

PART 1. HATSYIATSYA FOR ADZIDA

HIGH ATOKE

LOW ATOKE

LOW GANKOGUI

HIGH GANKOGUI

SONG

1st CANTOR
Go - ku - wo   be   to - hia - me   mie - le   be a - hɔ - ke - li - a   la - va -

2nd CANTOR
Fia - dza - wu   be

ADZIDA DANCE

ADZIDA DANCE

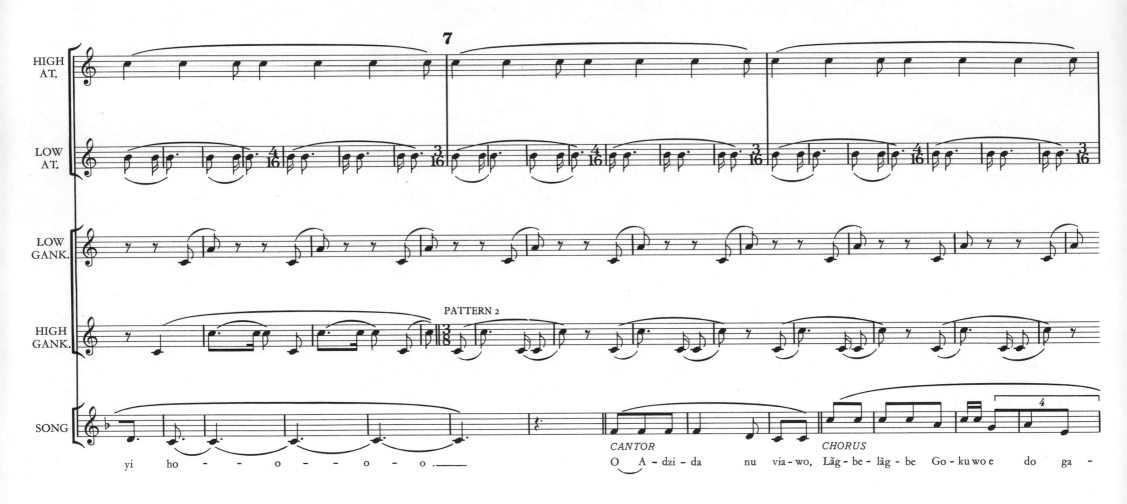

ADZIDA DANCE

9
11
HIGH AT.
LOW AT.
PATTERN B
LOW GANK.
HIGH GANK.
PATTERN 3
SONG
-le - le vɔ, A dzi - da - vi - awo mi - do gbe - da, ku me - toa nug - be a - ve - se - wo bla a - hɔ̃ -dzɔ-o, 'Agbo - hia mie - gba na a - vu - gbe - wo fe

ADZIDA DANCE

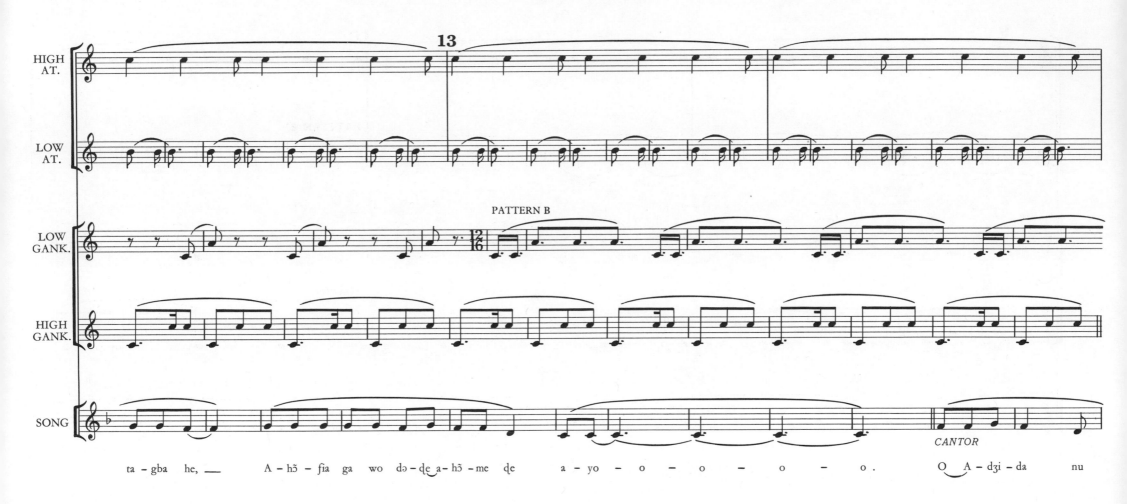

ta – gba he, ___ A – hɔ – fia ga wo dɔ – dǝ a – hɔ – me dǝ a – yo – o – o – o – o. O A – dʒi – da nu

ADZIDA DANCE

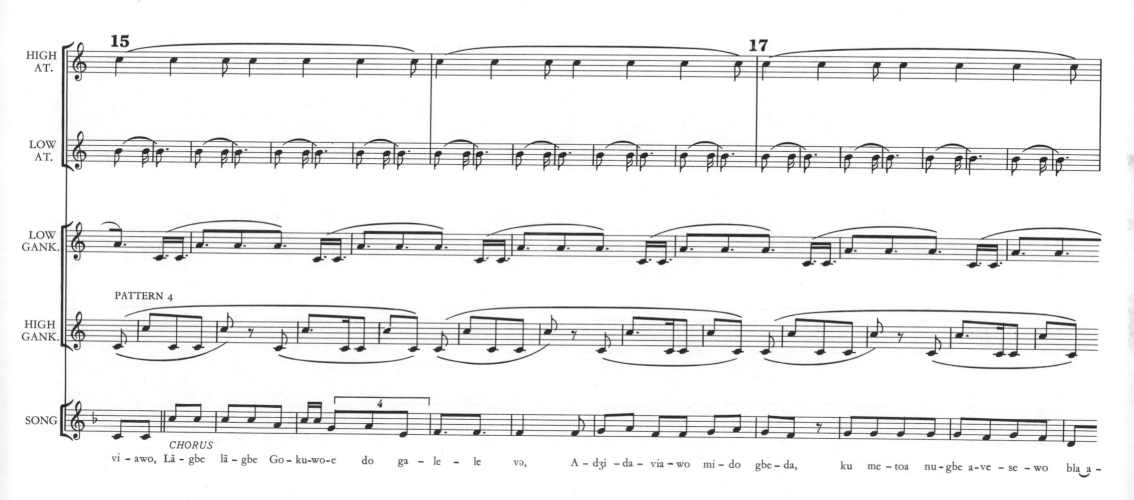

ADZIDA DANCE

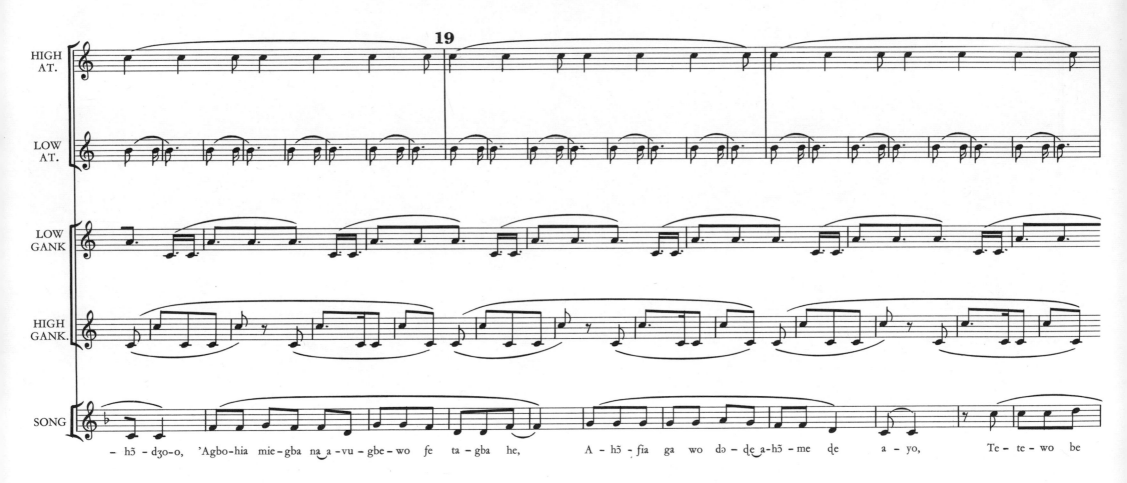

ADZIDA DANCE

ADZIDA DANCE

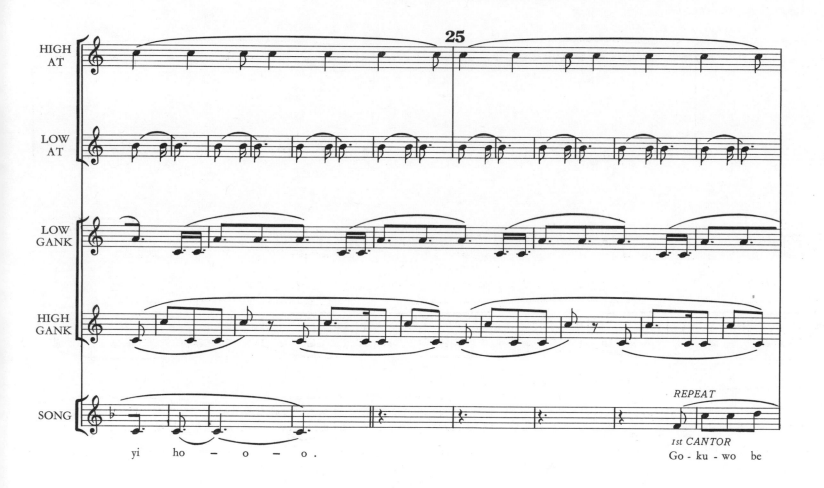

PART 2. AFÃƲU FOR ADZIDA

ADZIDA DANCE

ADZIDA DANCE

ADZIDA DANCE

ADZIDA DANCE

ADZIDA DANCE

ADZIDA DANCE

ADZIDA DANCE

ADZIDA DANCE

ADZIDA DANCE

ADZIDA DANCE

ADZIDA DANCE

ADZIDA DANCE

ADZIDA DANCE

ADZIDA DANCE

ADZIDA DANCE

ADZIDA DANCE

PART 3. THE ADZIDA DANCE

ADZIDA DANCE

82

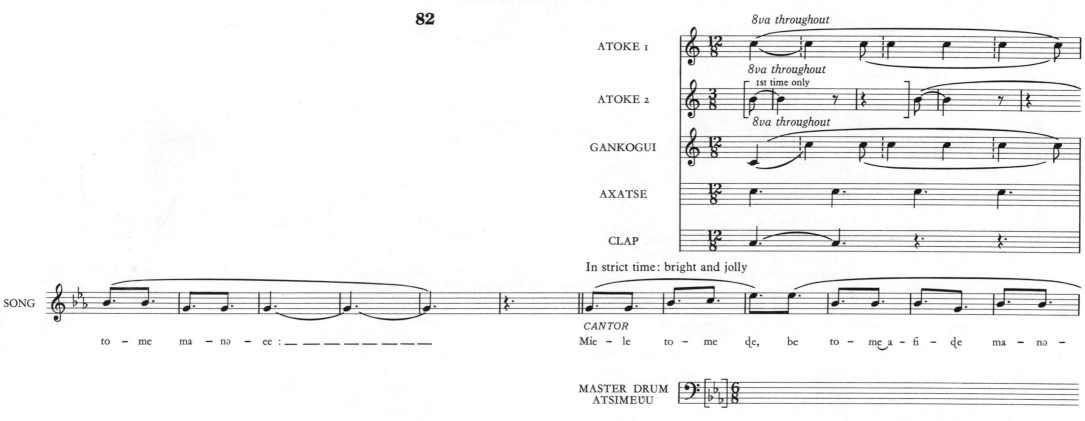

ADZIDA DANCE

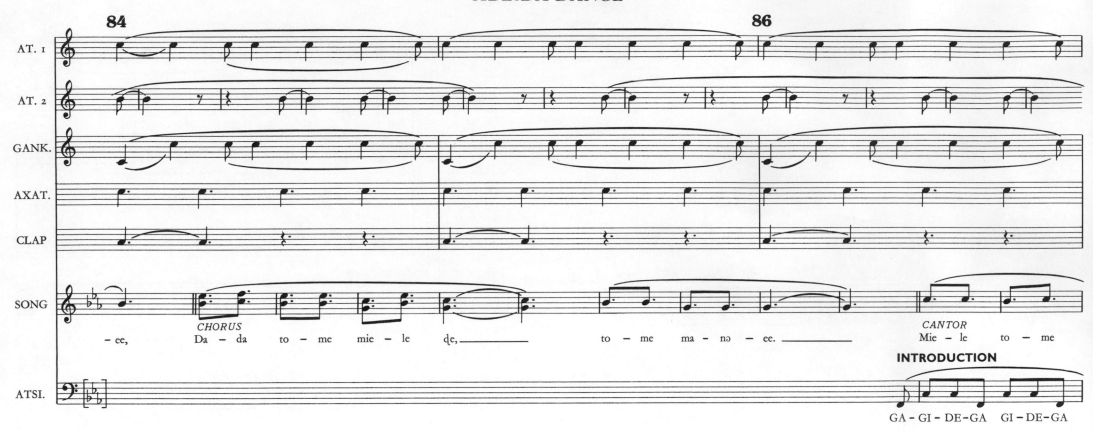

ADZIDA DANCE

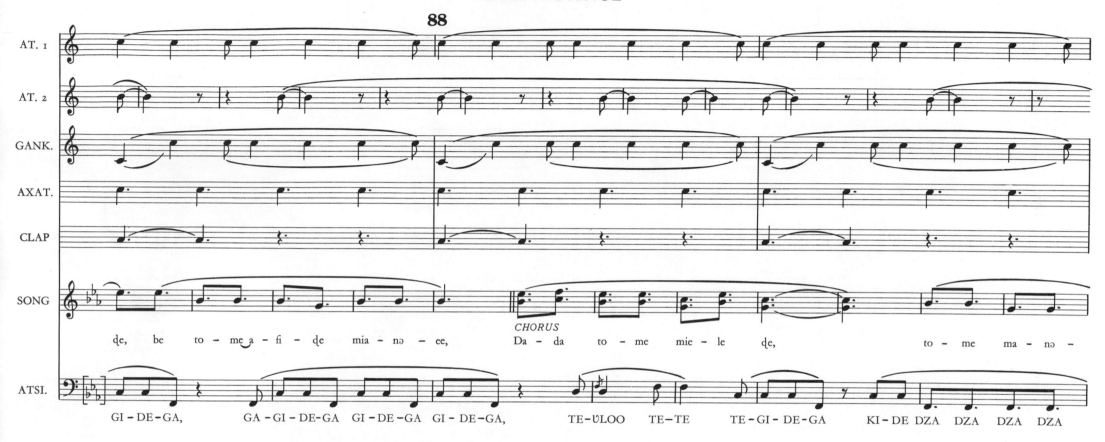

ADZIDA DANCE

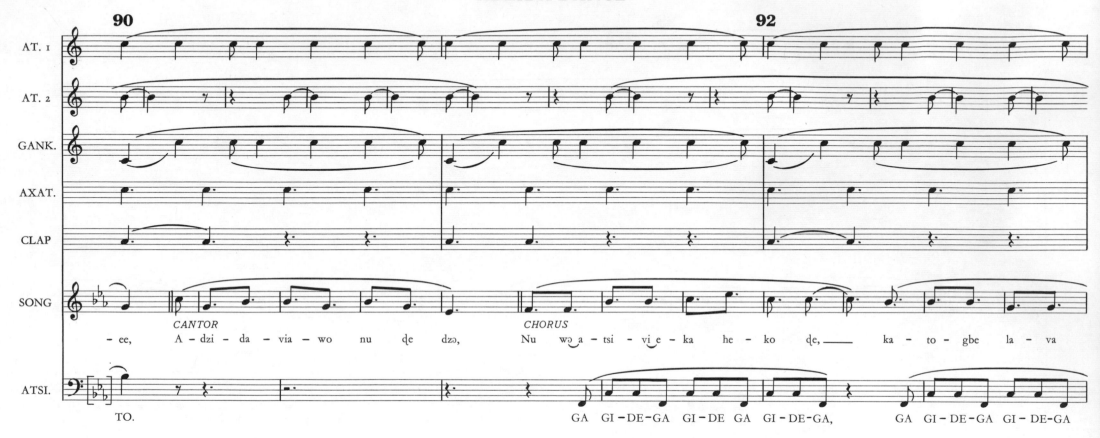

ADZIDA DANCE

ADZIDA DANCE

ADZIDA DANCE

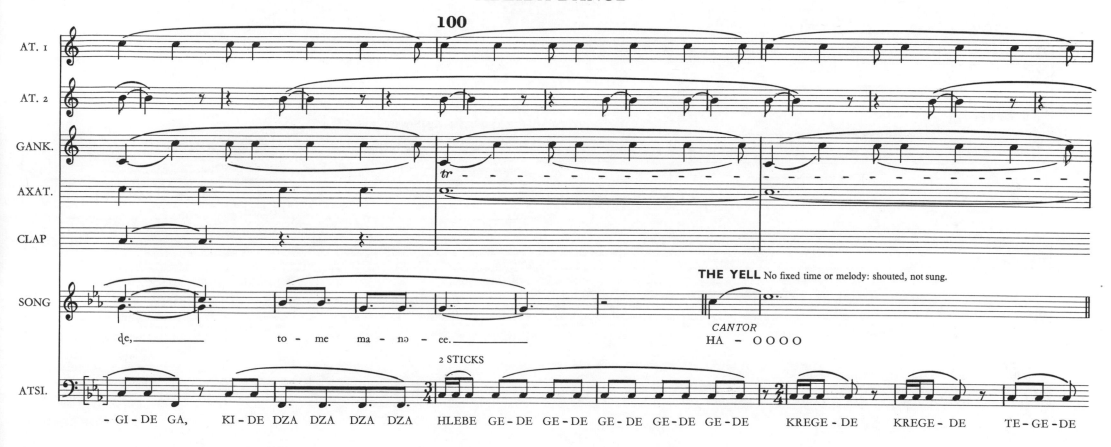

ADZIDA DANCE

ADZIDA DANCE

ADZIDA DANCE

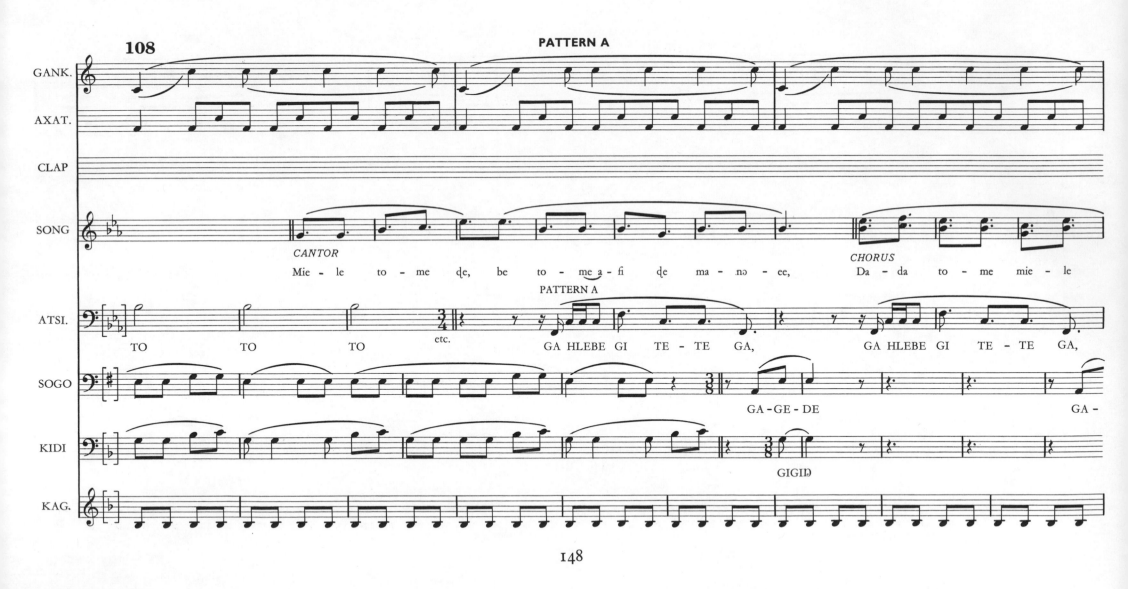

ADZIDA DANCE

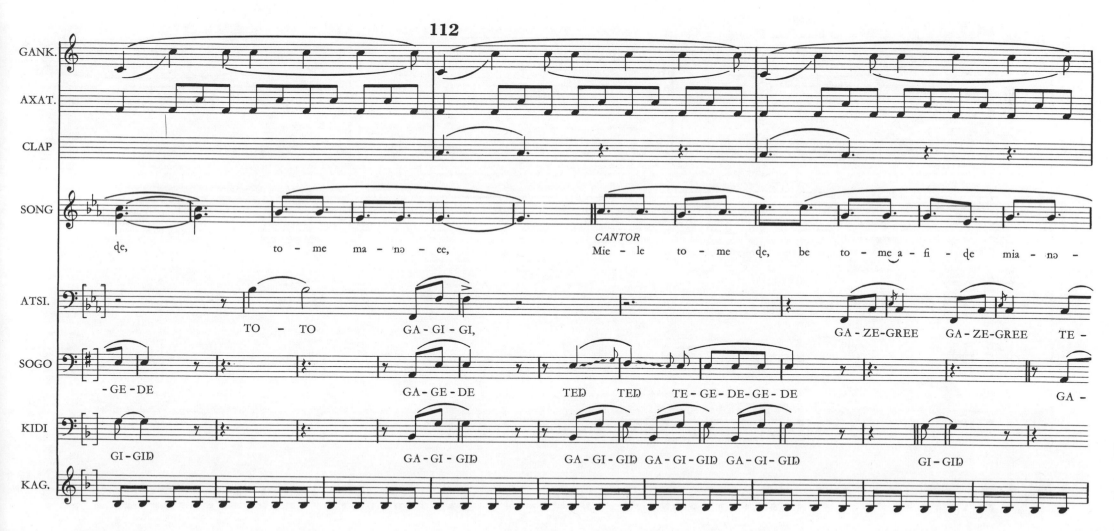

ADZIDA DANCE

ADZIDA DANCE

ADZIDA DANCE

ADZIDA DANCE

ADZIDA DANCE

ADZIDA DANCE

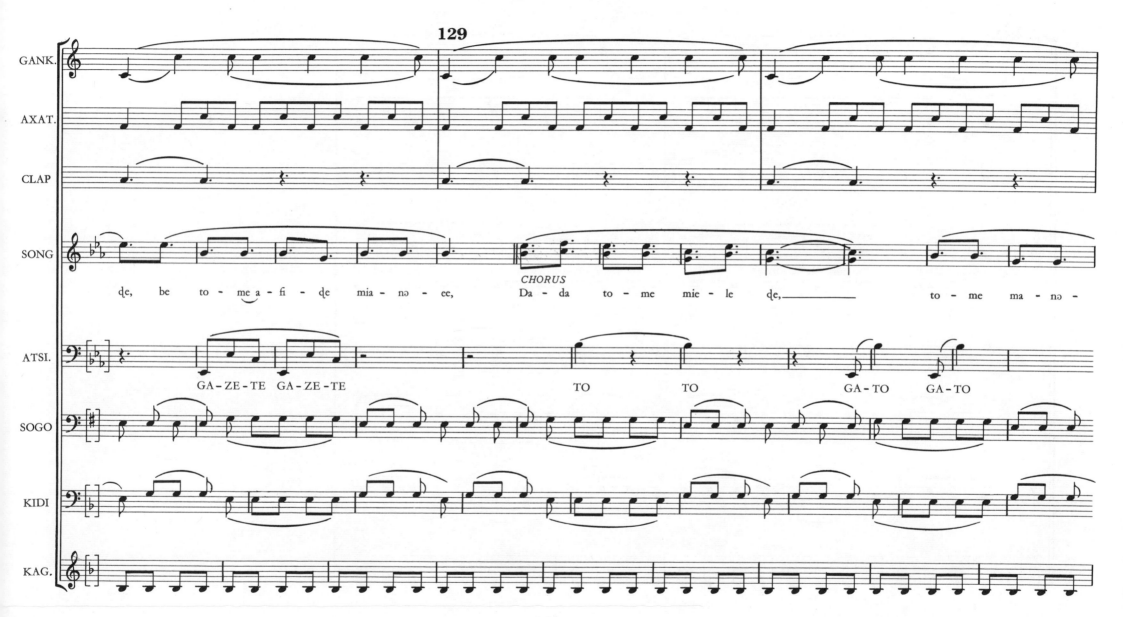

ADZIDA DANCE

ADZIDA DANCE

CANTOR

Mie – le to – me ɖe, be to – me a fi – ɖe ma – nɔ –

ADZIDA DANCE

ADZIDA DANCE

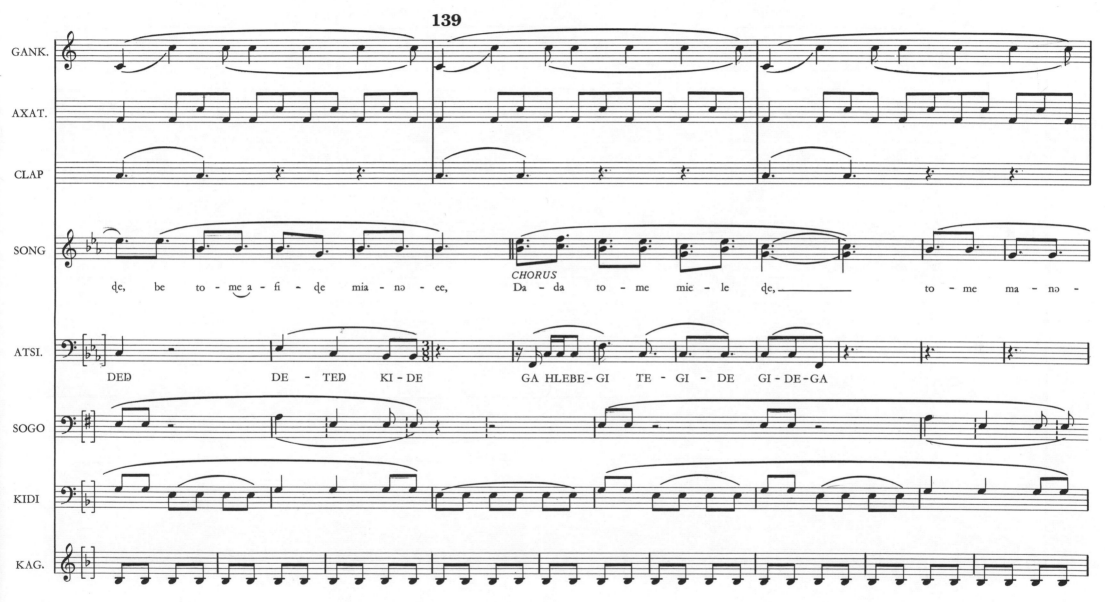

ADZIDA DANCE

ADZIDA DANCE

ADZIDA DANCE

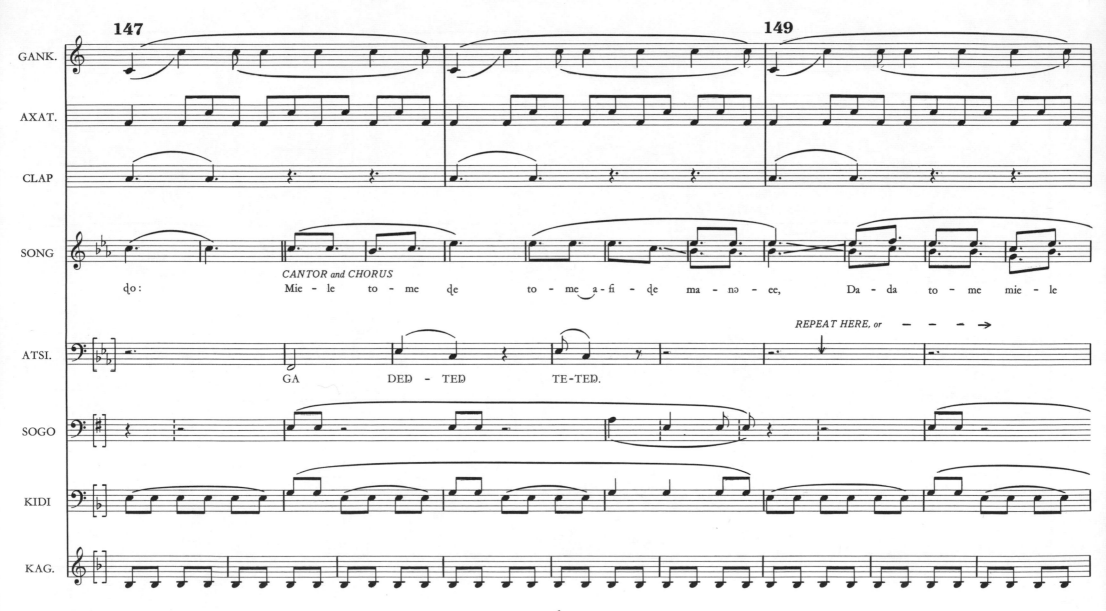

ADZIDA DANCE

CHANGING SIGNALS I.   **2.**

3.

AGBADZA SIGNAL & PRELIMINARY SONG

N. B. There is NO rhythmic relation between
song and drum in this section.

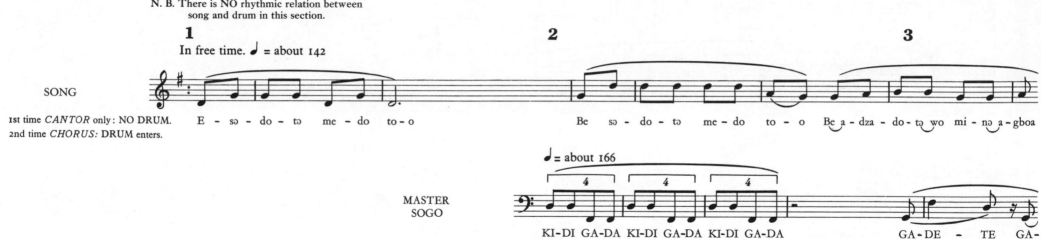

SONG

1st time *CANTOR* only: NO DRUM.
2nd time *CHORUS:* DRUM enters.

E - sɔ - do - tɔ   me - do   to - o   Be   sɔ - do - tɔ   me - do   to - o   Be a - dza - do - tɔ wo mi - nɔ a - gboa

MASTER
SOGO

KI-DI GA-DA KI-DI GA-DA KI-DI GA-DA   GA - DE - TE GA-

AGBADZA DANCE

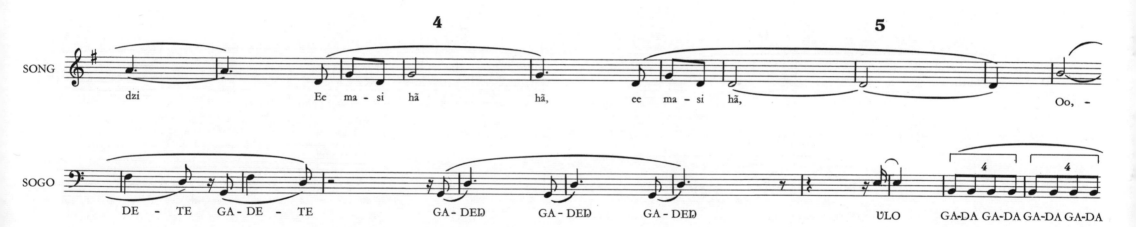

AGBADZA DANCE

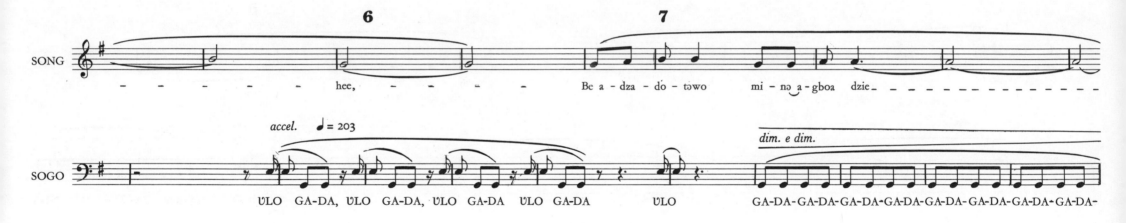

AGBADZA DANCE

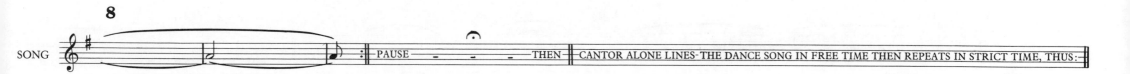

SONG

SOGO

GA-DA-GA-DA-GA-DA-GA-DA-GA-DA-GA-DA-GA-DA-GA-DA

AGBADZA DANCE

AGBADZA INTRODUCTION SIGNAL

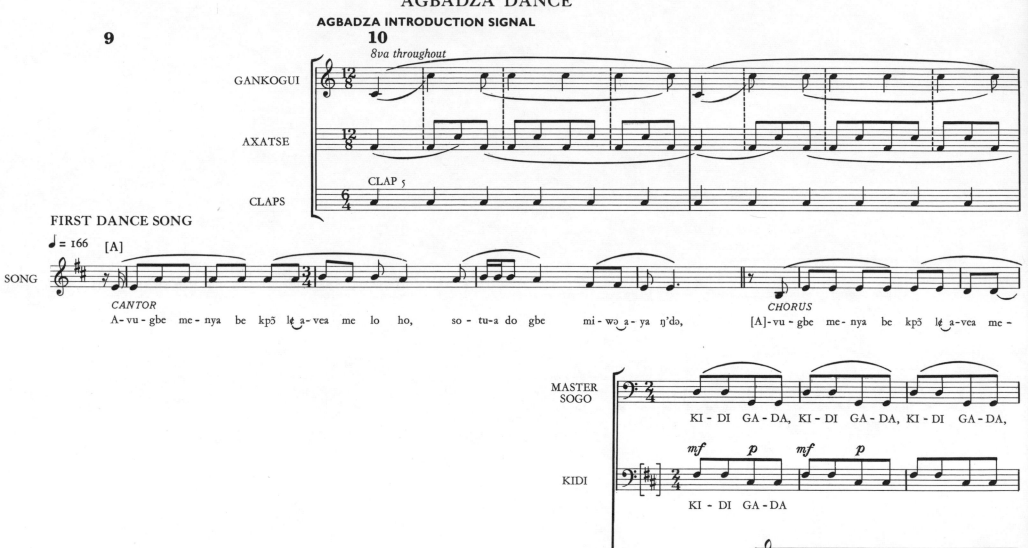

170

AGBADZA DANCE

AGBADZA DANCE

AGBADZA DANCE

173

AGBADZA DANCE

AGBADZA DANCE

AGBADZA DANCE

AGBADZA DANCE

VARIATIONS ON PATTERN A

AGBADZA DANCE

AGBADZA DANCE

AGBADZA DANCE

AGBADZA DANCE

AGBADZA DANCE

AGBADZA DANCE

AGBADZA DANCE

51

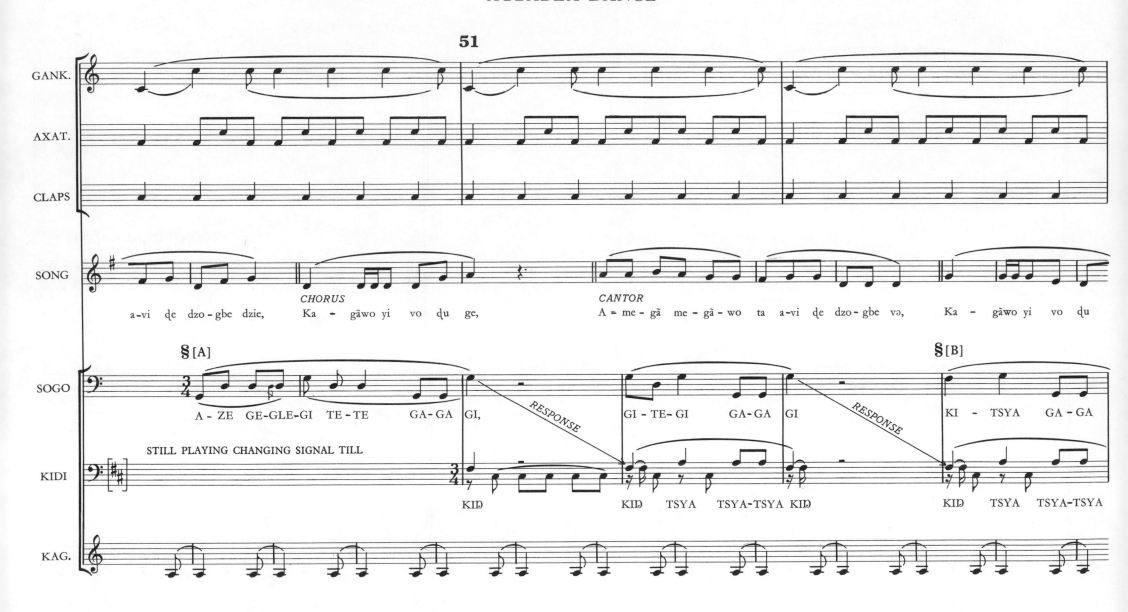

AGBADZA DANCE

AGBADZA DANCE

57

AGBADZA DANCE

AGBADZA DANCE

AGBADZA DANCE

AGBADZA DANCE

SECOND VARIATIONS ON PATTERN B

GANKOGUI

AXATSE

CLAPS

SONG

CANTOR
A - hɔ̃ - me su - ka - wo ta a-vi ɖe dzo-gbe dzie, Ka - gãwo yi vo ɖu

MASTER
SOGO

GI - TE - GI GA - GA

KIDI

KIꝊ TSYA TSYATSYA KIꝊ.

KAGAꝊ

KA - GAꝊ KA - GAꝊ

AGBADZA DANCE

AGBADZA DANCE

AGBADZA DANCE

AGBADZA DANCE

AGBADZA DANCE

AGBADZA DANCE

AGBADZA DANCE

AGBADZA DANCE

AGBADZA DANCE

AGBADZA DANCE

AGBADZA DANCE

0

AGBADZA DANCE

AGBADZA DANCE

AGBADZA DANCE

AGBADZA DANCE

AGBADZA DANCE

AGBADZA DANCE

AGBADZA DANCE

AGBADZA DANCE

209

AGBADZA DANCE

AGBADZA DANCE

AGBADZA DANCE

AGBADZA DANCE

AGBADZA DANCE

AGBADZA DANCE

AGBADZA DANCE

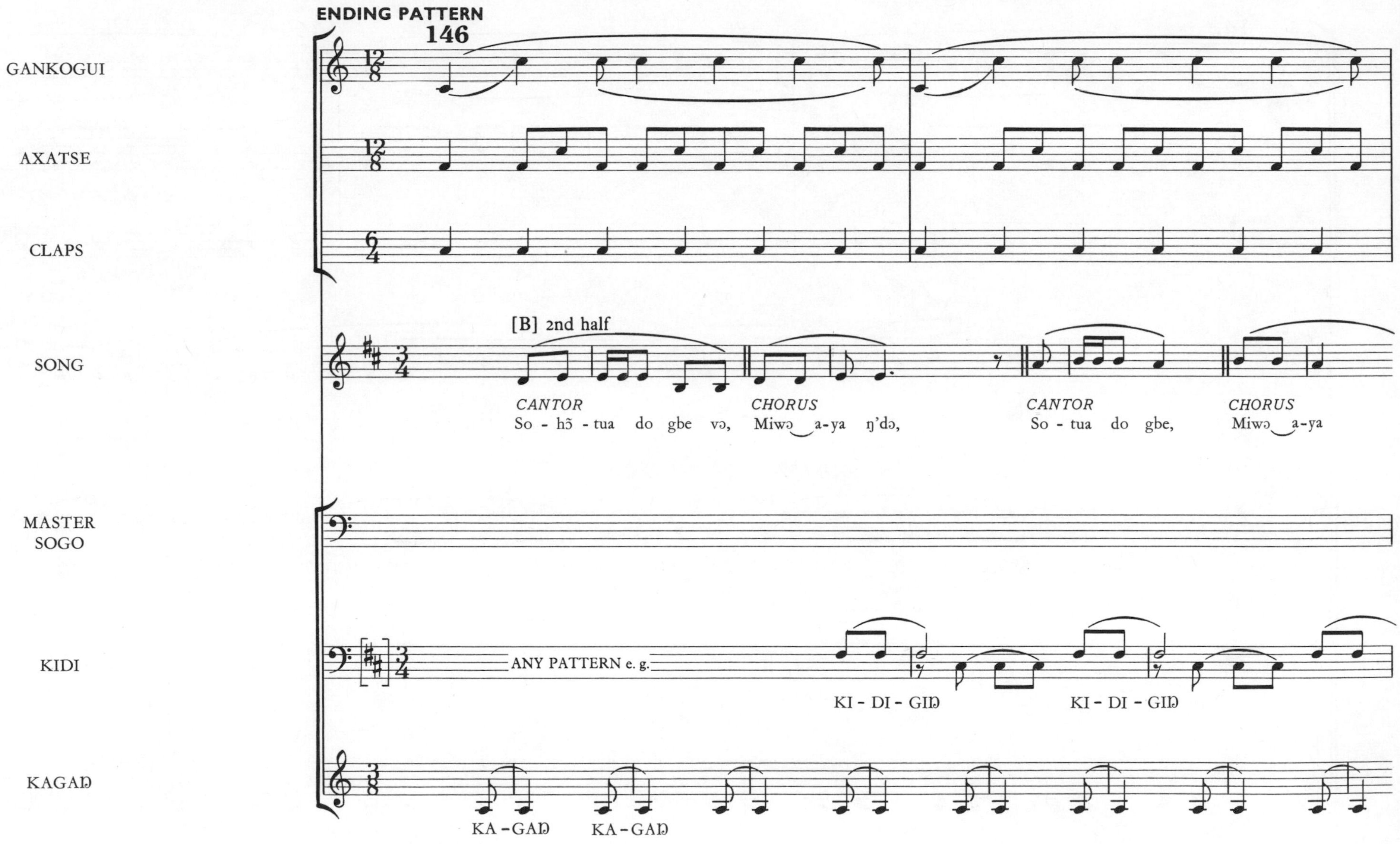

AGBADZA DANCE

P

ICILA DANCE

with West African (EWE TRIBE)
GANKOGUI pattern superimposed.

Lala Tribe — Northern Rhodesia

GANKOGUI

CLAP 1
CLAP 2

SONG

MASTER DRUM
IKULU

AKACHE

ICIBITIKU

MBA-LA   MBA-LA   MBA-LA PA - KU,

KA- BI - TI - KU   KA- BI - TI - KU

218

ICILA DANCE

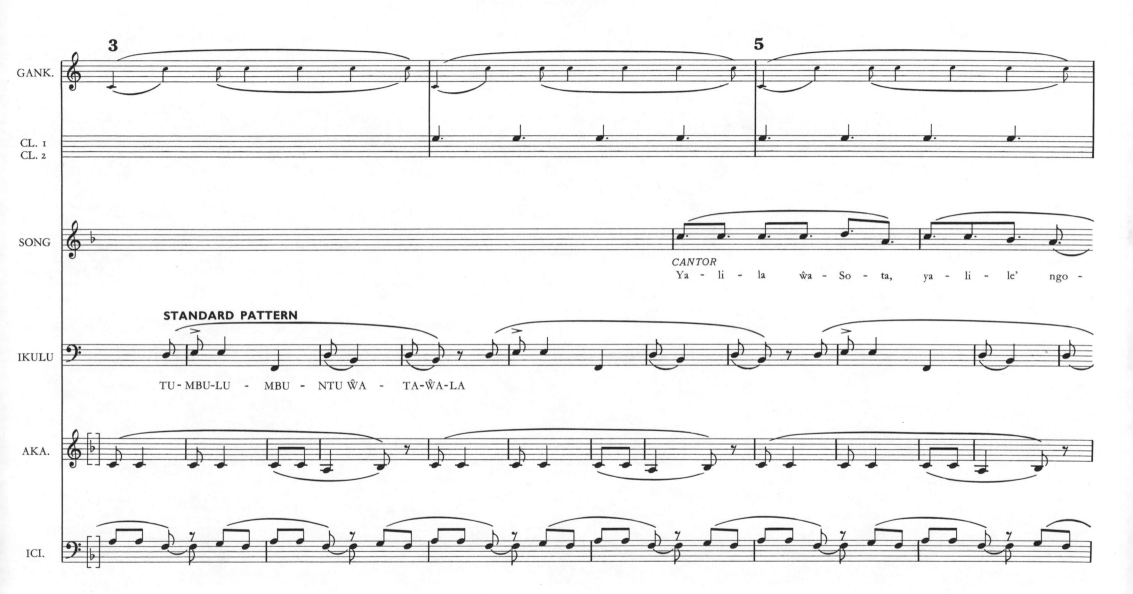

CANTOR
Ya - li - la ŵa - So - ta, ya - li - le' ngo -

STANDARD PATTERN

TU - MBU-LU - MBU - NTU ŴA - TA-ŴA-LA

ICILA DANCE

ICILA DANCE

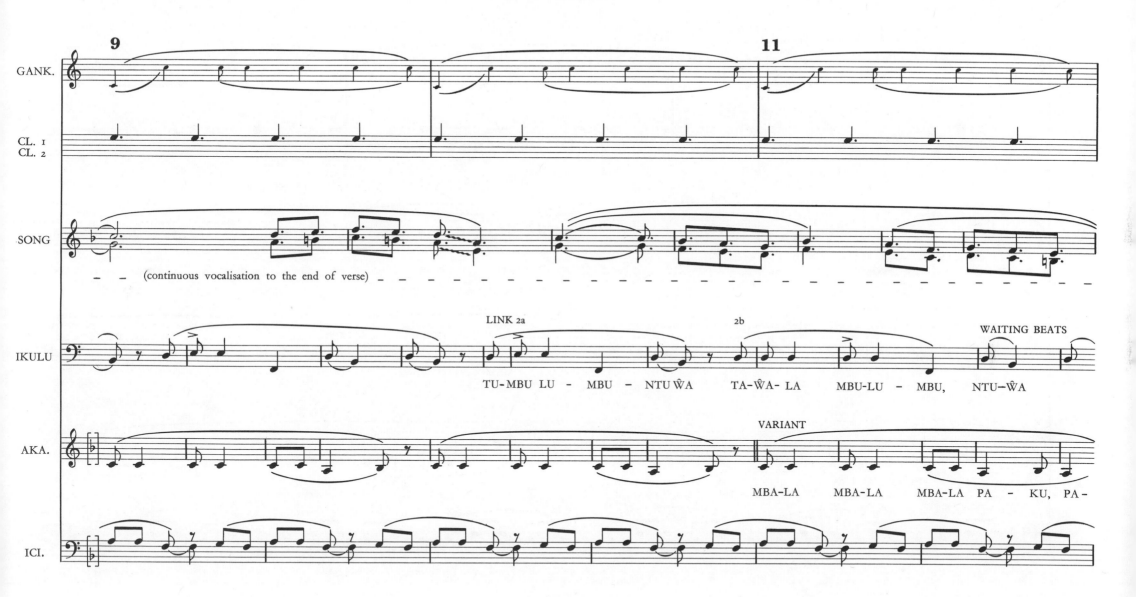

ICILA DANCE

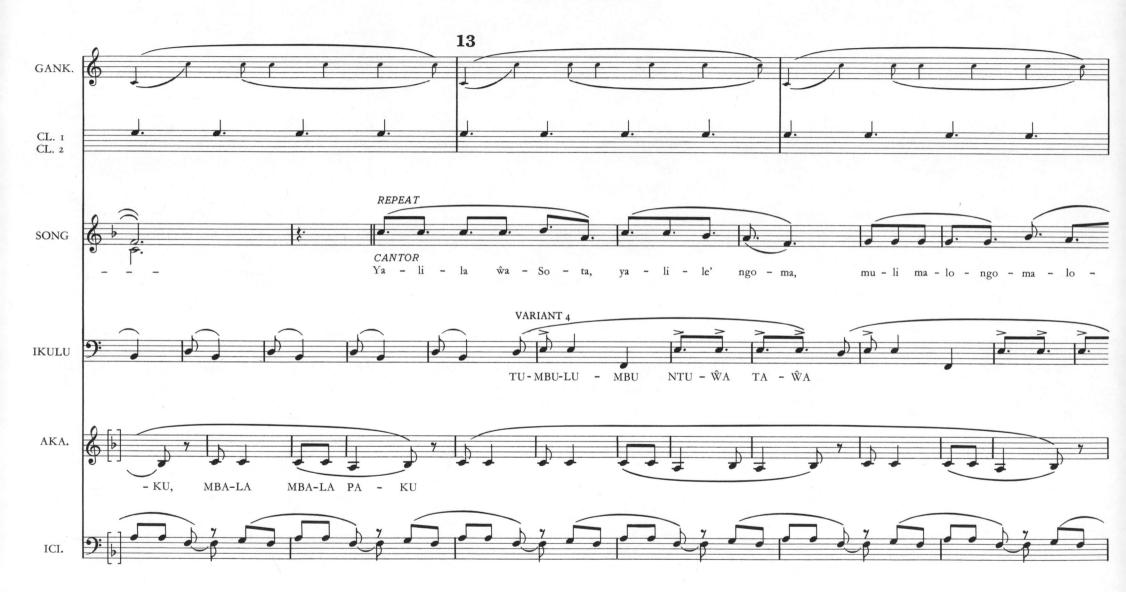

ICILA DANCE

ICILA DANCE

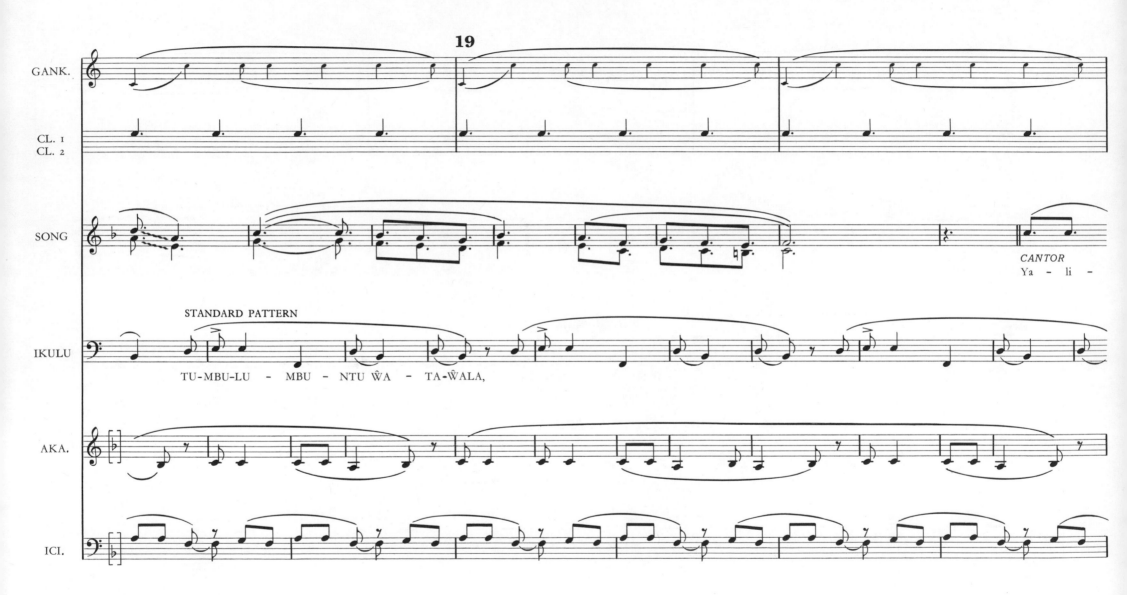

ICILA DANCE

225

ICILA DANCE

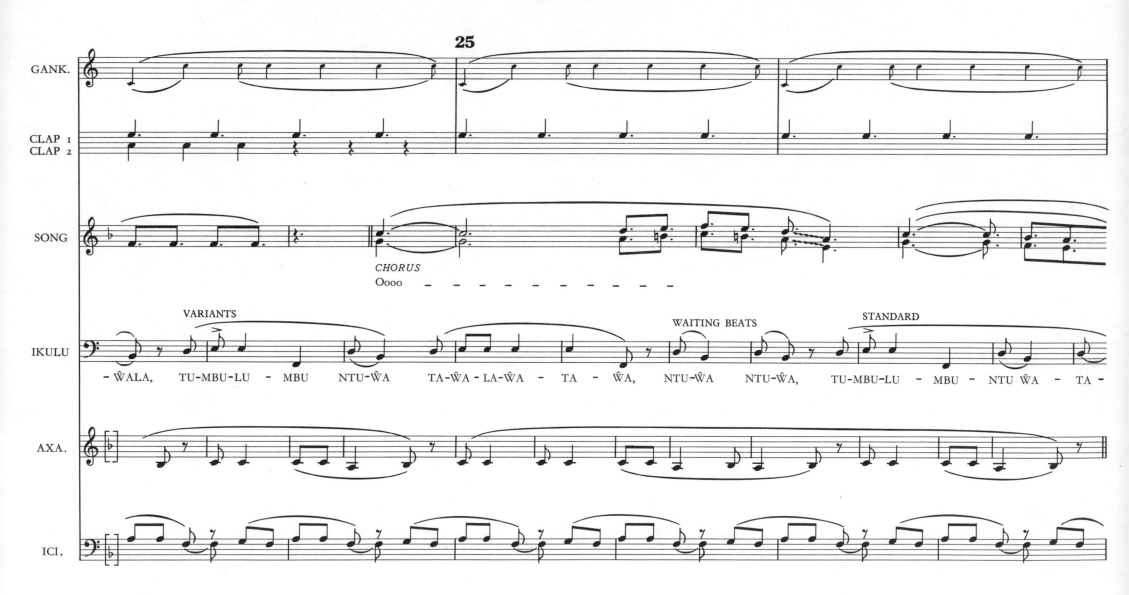

ICILA DANCE

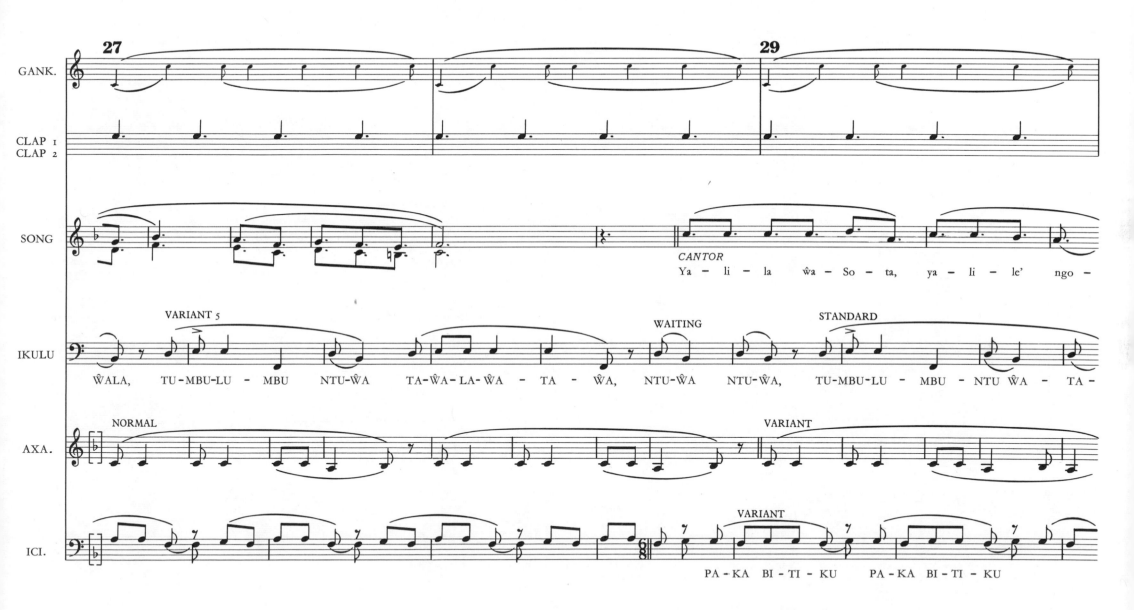

ICILA DANCE

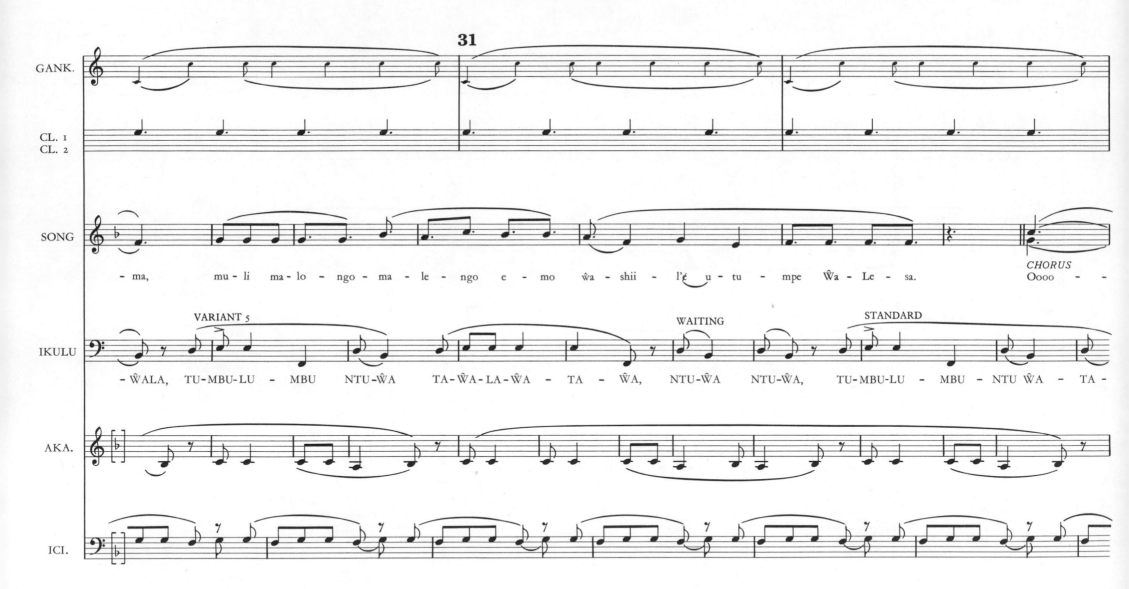

ICILA DANCE

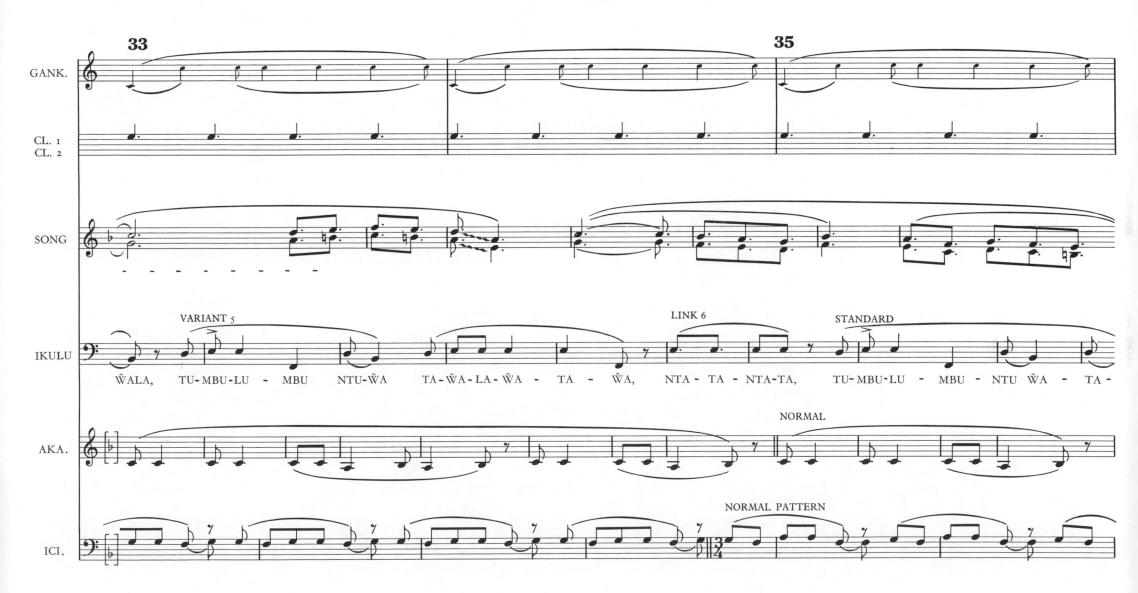

ICILA DANCE

ICILA DANCE

ICILA DANCE

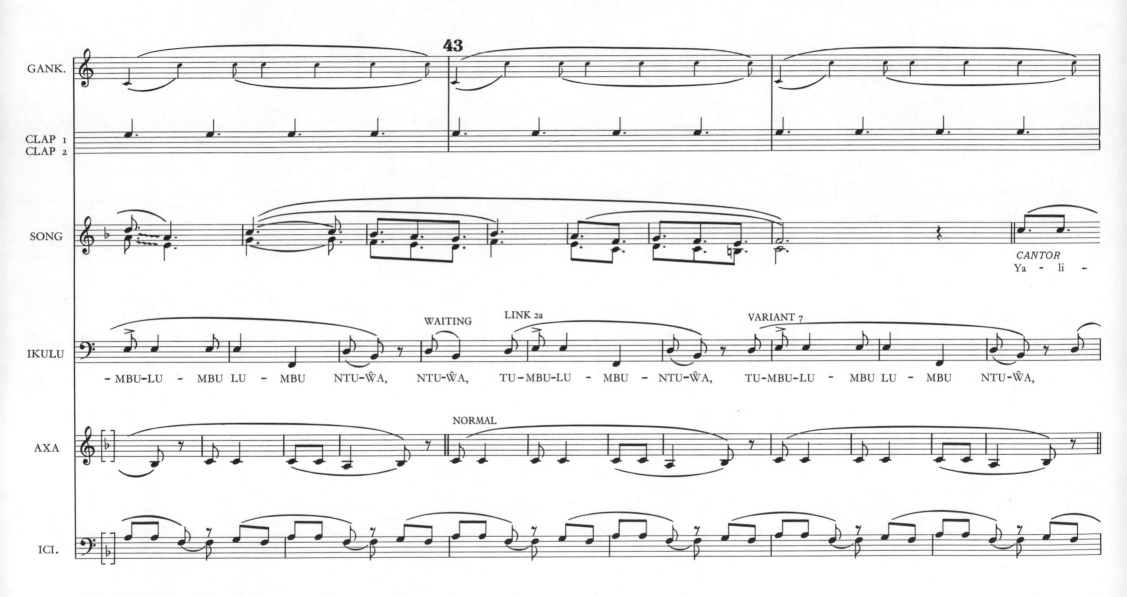

ICILA DANCE

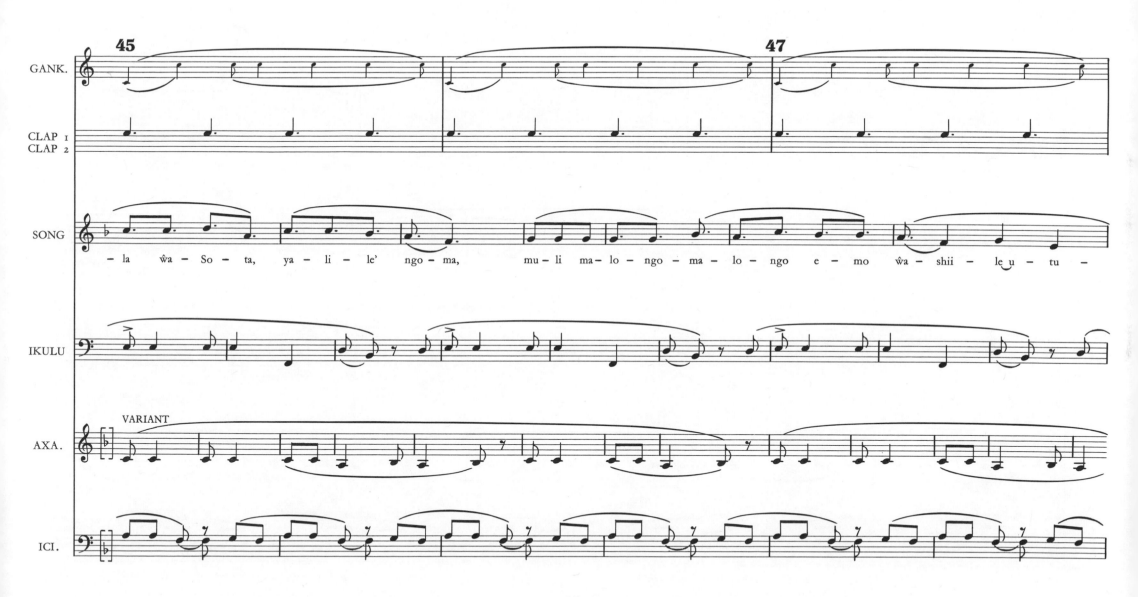

la — ŵa — So — ta, ya — li — le' ngo — ma, mu — li ma — lo — ngo — ma — lo — ngo e — mo ŵa — shii — le u — tu —

ICILA DANCE

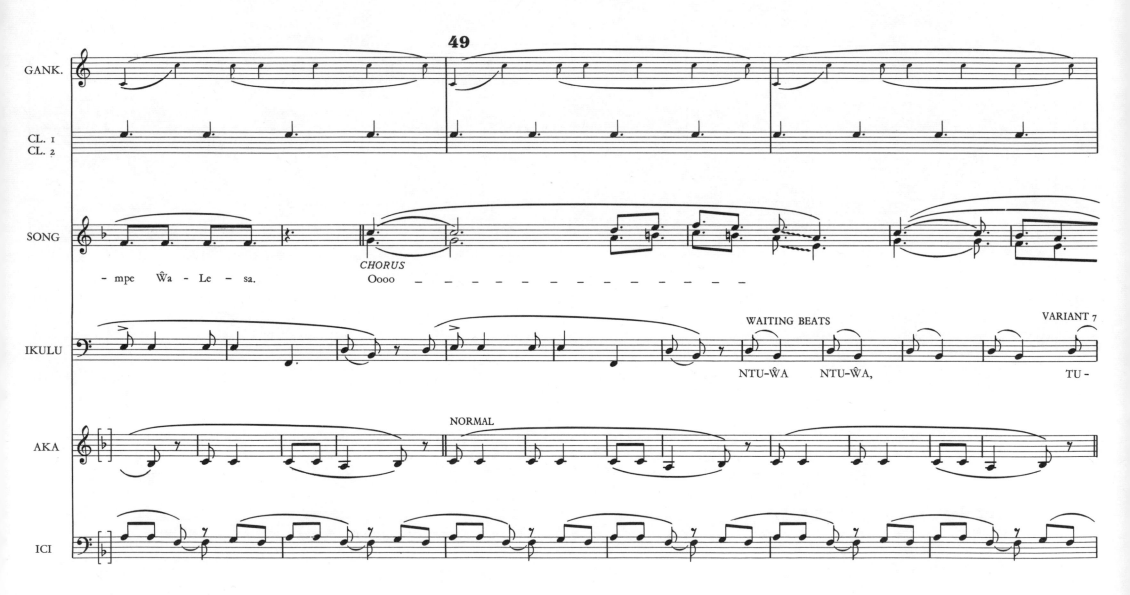

ICILA DANCE

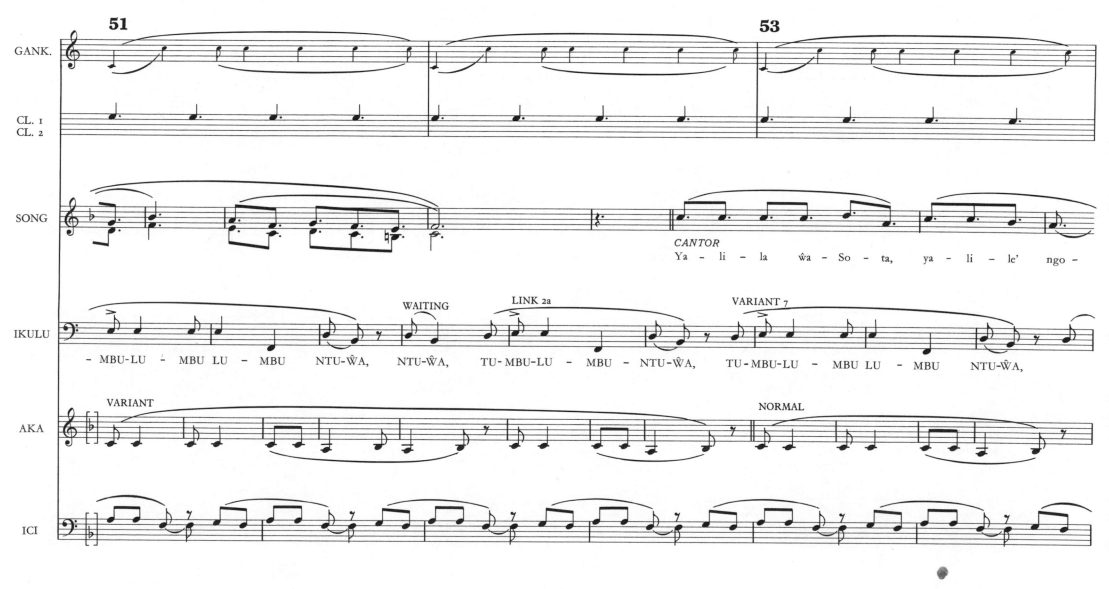

ICILA DANCE

APPENDIX

Two Independent Corroborators

NATALIE CURTIS: Songs and Tales from the Dark Continent (p. 98)

[1920] [*by permission of G. Schirmer Inc. New York. (Chappell & Co. Ltd., London)*]

Also on p. 98, for the song "Nyam'nje-nje," she gives the same clap in this form:

To show how the African thinks of it, we prefer to score this clap as:

APPENDIX

[1946]   *BROTHER BASILE:* **Aux Rythmes des Tambours** (p. 86) [*Reproduced by permission of Brother Basile*]

He gives the 'croisement des rythmes' of four drums thus:

Tableau II

REPRODUCED BY THE HALSTAN PROCESS
AND PRINTED BY HALSTAN & CO., LTD.,
AMERSHAM, BUCKS.